Physical Characteristics of the Staffordshire Bull Terrier

(excerpted from the American Kennel Club breed standard)

Body: Close coupled, with a level topline, wide front, deep brisket and well sprung ribs being rather light in the loins.

Tail: Undocked, of medium length, low set, tapering to a point and carried rather low.

Hindquarters: Should be well ı down with stifles well bent. I parallel when viewed from ł front.

Height at shoulder: 14 to 16 inches.

Weight: Dogs, 28 to 38 pounds; bitches, 24 to 34 pounds, these heights being related to weights.

Coat: Smooth, short aı

Staffordshire Bull Terrier

◇

By Jane Hogg Frome

Contents

Health Care of Your Staffordshire Bull Terrier   **103**

Discover how to select a qualified veterinarian and care for your dog at all stages of life. Topics include vaccination scheduling, skin problems, dealing with external and internal parasites and common medical and behavioral conditions.

Your Senior Staffordshire Bull Terrier   **127**

Consider the care of your senior Staffordshire Bull Terrier, including the proper diet for a senior. Recognize the signs of an aging dog, both behavioral and medical; implement a special-care program with your vet and become comfortable with making the final decisions and arrangements for your senior Stafford.

Showing Your Staffordshire Bull Terrier   **135**

Experience the AKC dog show world, including different types of shows, the basics of ring procedure and the making of a champion. Go beyond the conformation ring to obedience, agility and other competitive events.

Behavior of the Staffordshire Bull Terrier   **144**

Learn to recognize and handle common behavioral problems in your Staffordshire Bull Terrier, including barking, jumping up, aggression with people and other dogs, chewing, digging, separation anxiety, etc.

KENNEL CLUB BOOKS: STAFFORDSHIRE BULL TERRIER
ISBN: 1-59378-210-1

Copyright © 1999 • Revised American Edition: Copyright © 2004
Kennel Club Books, Inc., 308 Main Street, Allenhurst, NJ 07711 USA
Cover Design Patented: US 6,435,559 B2 • Printed in South Korea

Photography by:
Norvia Behling, Carolina Biological Supply, Kent and Donna Dannen, Wil de Veer, Doskocil, Isabelle Français, Tony George, James Hayden-Yoav, James R. Hayden, RBP, Bill Jonas, Dwight R. Kuhn, Dr. Dennis Kunkel, Mikki Pet Products, Phototake, Jean Claude Revy, Nikki Sussman, Theo von Sambeek, Dr. Andrew Spielman and C. James Webb.

Illustrations by Renée Low.

HISTORY OF THE

STAFFORDSHIRE BULL TERRIER

Mankind has enjoyed the faithfulness of the dog by his side for centuries. Few dogs desire to please their human masters as much as the Staffordshire Bull Terrier. Dogs in general have accommodated man and his every whim for many generations—anything to please the master. Today's Staffordshire Bull Terrier, in mind and body, echoes that sentiment with might and determination.

A SPECIALIST IN BODY AND MIND

Before the days of dog shows and the mating of pure-bred champions, humans recognized the merit of dogs that could specialize in performing a specific job or task. We bred dogs that could hunt, herd, haul, guard, run, track and perform countless other tasks geared toward making our human lives more comfortable, enjoyable and manage-

(Opposite page) A bold metaphor of Britain's spirit, the Staffordshire Bull Terrier represents the modern example of the bull and terrier dogs. This muscular beauty is called Wildstaff Nightmare.

Understanding the Staffordshire Bull Terrier as a pet requires knowledge of the dog's history as a baiting and fighting dog. No dog matches this breed's devotion in mind and body to its master.

> ## BRAIN AND BRAWN
> Since dogs have been inbred for centuries, their physical and mental characteristics are constantly being changed to suit man's desires for hunting, retrieving, scenting, guarding and warming their masters' laps. During the past 150 years, dogs have been judged according to physical characteristics as well as functional abilities. Few breeds can boast a genuine balance between physique, working ability and temperament.

The physical characteristics of a fighting dog still distinguish the Staffordshire Bull Terrier, including the pronounced cheek muscles, long legs and loose shoulders.

able. Each dog's anatomy reflected the tasks that man set before him. The hunting dog had an insulated coat, a super-sensitive nose, a short-coupled body, a deep chest and straight, strong legs. The coursing dog had longer legs, a tucked-up abdomen (for speed), a deep chest (for lung capacity), keen eyesight and a narrow, long muzzle (to slice the wind). The guard dogs were true heavyweights: massive and solidly boned with punishing jaws and nerves of steel.

The physical characteristics that set the Staffordshire Bull Terrier apart are its impressive musculature, strongly undershot strong jaws and large teeth, very pronounced cheek muscles, loose shoulders, roach back, low-slung body and long legs that bend in the forequarters. These are the characteristics of a fighting or baiting dog that enable him to perform the tasks

that the breed, indeed all the bull and terrier dogs, were created to tackle. The decree "Go low, pin and hold!" was in sooth a battle cry! This type of imposing physique was needed for the dogs to fight one another, as well as to dodge and grab an ornery bull with their powerful gripping jaws and hold on to it without being tossed aside!

Baiting a bull, an animal 20 or more times the size of a dog, placed some obvious demands on the dog and his anatomy and temperament. The desired temperament of a bull and terrier dog for baiting was not that of a vicious, risk-taking daredevil. Instead, the baiting dog required an even-keeled, level-headed, obedient temperament,

Although the Staffordshire Bull Terrier today doesn't pursue wild game like boar and bear, as its ancestors did, the American Bulldog (shown here) is still used on these risky pursuits.

The American Staffordshire Terrier, shown here, derived from Staffordshire Bull Terrier crosses to other terriers in the US.

peppered with patience, indomitable courage and tenacity. The bulldog excelled in the pinning and holding of a bull, but lacked the flexibility required in the dog pit. Thus, the smaller bull and terrier dogs were designed to take on this challenge and each other.

Imagine the heart of the dog that willingly undertakes such a task for the sake of pleasing his master! Baiting and fighting dogs were not the only kinds of dogs that risked their lives for their human counterparts. Indeed, herding and droving dogs, big-game hunting dogs and even the smaller terriers risked their lives for the sake of accomplishing their tasks. Nonetheless, the bloody endeavor of slaying a bull overshadows almost any other task set before a dog.

The original fighting-dog types were large, mastiff dogs with heavy, low-slung bodies and powerfully developed heads. Some accounts also describe the deep, frightening voice of the mastiff types. In appearance, the mastiffs were appalling and frightful. Mastiff dogs yielded not only fighting dogs but also flock guards, scenthounds and other powerful hunters. Consider the size and fearlessness of such modern-day mastiffs as the Great Pyrenees, Kuvasz, Dogo Argentino and Spanish Mastiff. Consider the size and features of the Bloodhound, Great Dane, Newfoundland and Polish Hound. All these dogs derive from crosses to these powerful mastiffs of yesteryear.

ORIGINAL PURPOSES OF THE GREAT MASTIFFS

Historians have recorded many impressive duties among the purposes of these original mastiffs.

Three modern-day breeds that derive from similar mastiff heritage: The Spanish Mastiff (upper left), shown here as an adolescent, is a powerful guard dog that can weigh three or four times more than a Stafford; the Dogo Argentino (upper right) has been called "a huge pit bull," developed in Argentina to hunt large game; and the Polish Hound (bottom) is a large scenthound with obvious mastiff influence.

Dogs used for war—armored, spiked and collared—became valuable weapons for humans trying to defend themselves from their enemies. These dogs were not only brave but also aggressive and resourceful. As early as 2100 BC, dogs were employed for warring purposes. Many famous kings and tribes used dogs to claim their victories. The dogs were trained in combat and were uniformed with impenetrable metal shields and spiked collars to protect them from their foes, who carried spears and other primitive weapons.

Spanning the millennia, Hammurabi, Kambyses, Varius and Henry VII were among the monarchs that valued dogs in their militia. These dogs were necessarily vicious and trusted no one except their one master. Appropriately, these war dogs were labeled *Canis bellicosus*.

The great mastiffs also assisted man by hunting large, ferocious game. These dogs commonly hunted in packs, maintained by the royals, and were used to pursue bison and aurochs in the wild forests. Dogs were also used to track the stag, considered noble game, as well as the wild boar, the most dangerous of wild game, notorious for its ruthless, nasty disposition. The mastiffs worked in conjunction with lighter, swifter dogs that tired the boar before the mighty mastiffs were released to slay it. Many men, dogs and horses were killed by wild boars fighting for their lives. There are accounts of boar dogs being kept in kennels 6,000 dogs strong. Today, mastiffs are rarely used for these purposes, but there are still boar hunts in the US, Germany and the Czech Republic.

Bear hunting was also a noble pursuit of the dogs of antiquity. The dogs were required to track the bear, corner it and keep it occupied until the hunters arrived with their firearms. The bear is a highly intelligent creature that could weigh over 750 lb and could easily outmatch a dog. Mastiffs in India produce the most colorful tales of hunting, including the pursuit of buffalo, leopards, panthers and elephants! Regardless of the actual truth of many of these accounts, the stories underscore the fearless tenacity of these mastiff dogs that are the ancestors of our Staffordshire Bull Terrier.

THE BULL AND TERRIER CROSS

The term "bull and terrier" refers to a common cross between bulldog types and the smaller terriers. Bulldogs during the mid-19th century did not resemble England's jolly Bulldog breed, whom we know and love today. The bulldogs of yore more closely resembled the taller, longer-headed dogs that we recognize as American Staffordshire Terriers or pit bulls. Experts purport that the terriers used in the early bull and terrier crosses were likely the Black and Tan Terrier, the progenitor of the Manchester Terrier of today; or perhaps the White English Terrier, a breed extinct in its original form but the forefather of the

modern Bull Terrier. These original bull and terrier crosses were desirable to create the smaller, agile and fearless canine needed for the "sport" of dog fighting. The larger mastiffs, while brave and heroic in battle and big-game hunting, were less successful in the pit. Unless a dog was suitably small, swift and flexible, he could not maneuver his way around a charging bull or another canine opponent. This is an age-old lesson that tends to evade many bulldog fanciers, especially those who insist that bigger is better. Even today, there are strains of American Pit Bull Terrier that are so large that they exceed 120 pounds. The question of size in the Staffordshire Bull Terrier would continue to be an issue for many years.

THE STAFFORDSHIRE TERRIER IN ENGLAND

The Staffordshire Terrier's forefathers were the companions of the working class in the "Black

though obviously more lethal a game, the breeders used the dog pit to determine who the "champions" were, so that only the "gamest" dogs of all would produce the next generation of fighting dogs.

The term "game" applies to the most desirable attribute of a bull and terrier. Gameness indicates that the dog will fight fearlessly to the death and never think of quitting. It is this tenacity for which breeders strived in their bull and terriers. Likewise, game-bred pit bulls today are still tested in the pit despite the illegality and the risks involved. Dog fighters employ the terminology "scratch" to indicate how many times in a fight a dog cowers or tries to exit the pit.

Not until the 1930s did fanciers in England attempt to establish the Staffordshire Terrier as a separate breed and begin to imagine their dogs competing outside the dog pit.

The American Pit Bull Terrier embodies many of the same characteristics as the Stafford, although it does not enjoy the same level of recognition by the kennel clubs.

Country" in Stafford, England. In this part of England, bull and terriers were bred with great intensity, and owners continued to match their dogs in the pit long after dog fights were outlawed. Hardcore Stafford dogmen believed that the dog pit was the only true test of their dogs' worth and perceived these matches as "working tests" to determine which dogs were worthy of being bred. This mentality corresponds note for note with the show world's perspective of using the show ring to determine which dogs should be bred. Becoming a champion in the show world is assuredly a challenge, and only those dogs that prove themselves in the show ring deserve to be bred. Likewise,

> **HALF AND HALF**
> The bull and terrier cross, regarded as a breed by some, was sometimes called "Half and Half." This nickname reflects the combination of the bulldog and terriers that were used to create this type of dog. As time went on, fanciers argued over the desired proportion of bull and terrier in the breed. The Staffordshire Bull Terrier has considerably more bulldog in it than does the Bull Terrier or American Staffordshire Terrier, though the relationship between all of these dogs is evident.

While dog fighting was outlawed before this time, fights were still routinely held in a more-or-less clandestine fashion. It was around this time that the dog-fighting activities were actually abolished through police intervention, and by 1930 the law began to be fully enforced.

For the sake of establishing the breed and entering dog shows, the original standard, based on the superb show winner Jim The Dandy, owned by Jack Barnard, was drafted by the very committed breeder Joe Dunn. It was adopted in 1935 at the first meeting of the UK's Staffordshire Bull Terrier Club. It was subsequently recognized by England's Kennel Club later that year, and the breed was allowed to enter dog shows. The original club was established by more than 40 breeders, and Jack Barnard was the first president.

The dogs were first shown at the Hertfordshire Agriculture Society in June of 1935, just one

Does this look like the face of a fighter? Despite the breed's background, Staffords are known for their friendly nature and affectionate devotion to their families.

month after the club's establish-
ment. The following year, Cross
Guns Johnson, owned by Joe Dunn,
won the class at the prestigious
Crufts Dog Show, the first time the
Stafford was entered. Gentleman
Jim was the first champion with
The Kennel Club; he won his first
Challenge Certificate at the
Birmingham National Show. He
earned his championship in double
time—in just two shows! The first
championship show for Staffords,
held by the Southern Counties
Staffordshire Bull Terrier Society,
attracted 300 dogs in June of 1946.

The pioneers of the breed, who
lived in England's Black Country,
were not pleased with the entrance
of the Stafford into the show world.
They feared that the temperament
of the breed would be endangered
and that the true heart of the breed
would be lost. Many of these
pioneers continued to fight their
game Staffords to keep the "heart"
in their blood.

Another controversy emerged
concerning the desired size of the
dogs. In the original standard, the
size was similar to the more popular Bull Terrier, 15 to 18 inches.
Breeders were producing Staffords
that were too heavy and not mobile,
so by 1948 the height diminished to
14 to 16 inches. This change was
not welcomed by many breeders,
and dogs today still push the height
requirement of the standard.

In modern times, breeders have
concerned themselves with achiev-

The Bull Terrier,
distinguished by
its unique head
shape, is a taller,
heavier dog
than the Stafford.
Both breeds
derived from bull
and terrier crosses.

ing the perfect head on their
Staffordshire Bull Terriers. It is fair
to say that the head of the breed has
received too much emphasis and
the hindquarters and shoulders
have suffered, resulting in movement that is far from ideal in most
dogs.

THE STAFFORD GOES TO THE UNITED STATES

Many British industrial and mine
workers opted to immigrate to the
United States in the 1860s and
1870s. These hardworking Britons
brought their Staffordshire Bull
Terriers with them and resumed
breeding them in the US, often
crossing them with other terrier
types. These dogs became known as
Yankee Terriers, American Bull
Terriers and American (Pit) Bull
Terriers (as if placing parentheses

around the "pit" would soften the blow). These dogs were admired by the American public and revered for their devotion to family and children. Although not the size of most guard dogs, these dogs compared in courage and determination.

These dogs were also used in dog fights, as were many similar dogs that arrived with Irish immigrants. The United Kennel Club (UKC) was established as a registry for these pit bull dogs, which were refused acceptance by the larger American Kennel Club (AKC). The AKC did not grant the American Pit Bull Terrier recognition, though it would later recognize the same dog under the name of the Staffordshire Terrier in 1936.

The first Staffordshire Terrier registered with the AKC was Wheeler's Black Dinah. Many fanciers took advantage of the situation and dual-registered their dogs as Staffordshire Terriers with the AKC and as American (Pit) Bull Terriers with the UKC. (To further confuse matters, the American Dog Breeders Association, a national association for dogmen of the pit variety, registered the breed as the Staffordshire Terrier in the late 1930s.)

The Staffordshire Terrier Club of America was formed on May 23, 1936 to protect "The Grand Old Breed" formerly known as the American (Pit) Bull Terrier or Yankee Terrier. The standard was drawn up right away and Staffordshire Terriers entered the show rings. The first American shows at which the breed was exhibited

were held in conjunction with the International Kennel Club of Chicago in the late 1930s and as many as 50 dogs were exhibited. The first AKC champion of record was Maher's Captain D, who garnered the title in 1937. Arguably the most famous Staffordshire Terrier of this early period was Ch. X-Pert Brindle Biff, owned and bred by Clifford A. Ormsby.

As the gap of type variation expanded to a grand canyon within the breed, breeders decided to split the Staffordshire Terrier into two breeds. In 1972, the American Staffordshire Terrier was recognized, and two years later, the Staffordshire Bull Terrier reappeared on the scene. Employing the same name used by Joe Dunn in England in the 1930s, the Staffordshire Bull Terrier is the shorter legged, thicker dog, weigh-

A young white Staffordshire Bull Terrier. Although not as commonly seen, solid white is an allowable color according to the AKC breed standard.

ing 24 to 38 pounds and standing 14 to 16 inches tall. The American Staffordshire Terrier stands on longer legs and is 17 to 19 inches in height. Of course, the Staffordshire Bull Terrier in America still resembled the conformation of the original British dogs. Since the type of dog that became known as the American Staffordshire Terrier had no following in England, there was no similar controversy or dissension among fanciers. Although recognized as two distinct breeds (three, if you're inclined to include the UKC's American Pit Bull Terrier), these dogs are genetically similar, though the lines haven't been crossed in many generations.

This Staffordshire Bull Terrier possesses an impressive expansive chest and the desired musculature that is characteristic of the breed.

Some Staffordshire Bull Terrier owners are very passionate about their dogs. What more appropriate tribute to the breed than to tattoo its image on your arm!

CHARACTERISTICS OF THE
STAFFORDSHIRE BULL TERRIER

PERSONALITY AND TEMPERAMENT

For all the blood-curdling history of the Stafford, many astounding positive qualities permeate through every pore of the breed. The Staffordshire Bull Terrier is defined not only by its "indomitable courage and tenacity" but also by its unflinching affection for children. At first glance, such qualities appear contradictory. How could a formidable, fearless fighter be expected to curl up with the children at sundown? Who could expect that a dog bred to kill other dogs would be the choice of thousands of dog lovers around the world and be trusted with their children?

To understand this contradiction, the reader must identify which qualities in the Staffordshire Bull Terrier inspired the animal to undertake the Battle Royal, the fight to the death with a fellow canine. The quality is pure and simple: absolute devotion to mankind. No breed on earth desires to please its human owner more than the Stafford! The tenacity and courage of the breed are equally matched by its love of humans and its desire to please them. Staffords also recognize the tenderness and frailty of children, which inspires their dedication to and protection of them.

Historically, the Staffordshire Bull Terrier has earned the pet names the "Children's Nursemaid" or the "Nanny Dog," celebrating the breed's fondness of children. Owners must understand, though, that children should never be left unsupervised with any dog, regardless of the dog's size or temperament. Given the breed's stoic nature and resistance to pain, the Stafford can tolerate being handled by kids. Nevertheless, children must be properly instructed to handle a

Staffordshire Bull Terriers are devoted, loyal and caring companions. They usually get along famously with children.

The original "Nanny Dog," the Stafford is a fun-loving dog that makes a loving, protective pet. A special bond is formed between a Stafford puppy and child who grow up together.

dog. Children's natural exuberance can sometimes promote mistreating a dog, even if unintentionally.

Another quality endears the Stafford breed to children: its love of fun. The Stafford is an active, athletic and often silly dog. His comical antics and games of chase and fetch delight the likes of children and adults.

There is no doubt about the athletic abilities of a Staffordshire Bull Terrier. Just a mere glance at the dog's musculature, from head to toe, reveals that this is an active person's choice. The cheeks are prominently muscled, giving the dog incredible holding strength with his jaws. Many owners provide their dogs swinging ropes and even tires for exercise. The dog's feet are well padded and strong, connected to an athlete's muscular legs. Have you ever seen a Stafford in mid-air? What amazing strength and balance this little terrier possesses! When a Stafford flexes, whether he's pouncing vertically

upward or just smiling, it's a joy to behold!

The Staffordshire Bull Terrier puts his muscle where his pearly whites are: this is an unstoppable watchdog for family and property. For his pounds, the Stafford ranks first among the guard dogs, as he is the smallest of the capable canine defenders. While many of his relatives, the Mastiff, Bullmastiff and Boxer, for example, stand many inches taller than the Stafford, the breed compensates with its solid strength and unshakeable devotion to those it is protecting. A bullet doesn't need to be large to be effective: the Staffordshire Bull Terrier, perfectly aimed and propelled, can stop a would-be perpetrator in

Stafford puppies are exuberant dogs with a true sense of comic timing. They give as much pleasure to their spectators as to their playmates.

A tire swing makes a marvelous form of entertainment for the Stafford. This conditioned athlete is showing off his agility and the superior strength of his jaw.

Though not retrievers by trade, talented Staffords never cease to amaze their owners with their repertoire of skills.

his tracks. Tenacity and strength are intermingled to make this dog fearless and formidable. Keep in mind, however, that the Stafford is not a true guard dog; unlike the Doberman Pinscher and Bullmastiff, the breed was not designed as a protector.

Is every Staffordshire Bull Terrier friendly, trustworthy and even-tempered? Breeders will contend that most Staffords do possess these qualities in spades, though not all. Friendliness should indeed define the breed, though most breeds and most dogs should be friendly. Many breed standards include the word "friendly" in the description of the Stafford's characteristics. The

AKC breed standard also includes the words "trustworthy stability," assuring the reader that the Staffordshire Bull Terrier is beyond reliable in the ideal circumstances. The standard even makes mention of the breed's special affection toward children. Provided that the dog has been properly reared and socialized, there should be no question regarding the friendliness and reliability of the dog. However, obviously dogs that are not treated kindly, trained and raised with intelligence and responsibility cannot be as consistently dependable.

The evenness of the Stafford's temperament stems in part from

A highly recommended way to send Christmas greetings! Here's Wildstaff Nightmare masquerading as an elfin wonder.

the breed's history in the dog pit. Dog fighters raised and bred dogs to be completely predictable. These are powerful, tenacious, aggressive dogs that must be totally reliable. As disturbing as the image may be, the owner of the losing Staffordshire Bull Terrier in a dog fight had to trust his dog enough, even when the dog was mangled and in pain, to be able pick the dog up and treat his wounds. These dogs, often in shock as well as horrific pain, never attempted to bite their masters. Such dogs were strictly dog-aggressive, never people-aggressive, even in dire, unfathomable circumstances.

That's why your four-year-old can step on your Staffordshire Bull Terrier's toes without the dog's reacting defensively. That's why the family cat can swat at your Stafford's tail and get no reaction except a yawn. A dog that would sacrifice his well-being, in fact his life, for his owner's satisfaction is a dog that could be relied upon in any situation.

Staffords are adaptable but sensitive. You cannot mistreat a Stafford. These dogs should not be harshly reprimanded nor unfairly dismissed. They live to please their owners, and nothing is as crushing to a Staffordshire Bull Terrier as his owner's anger or displeasure. While firmness and fairness should define your treatment of a Stafford, the dog must always sense that you are pleased with his actions. Praise to a Stafford is nothing short of glorious.

The Stafford's sensitivity can only be present in a dog of extreme intelligence. Staffordshire Bull Terriers tend to be adept problem-solvers, possessing powers that border on reasoning. They are tenacious and patient, rarely tiring over a challenge.

Staffordshire Bull Terriers can adapt to practically any situation and handle whatever tasks and challenges are set before them, provided the owner treats the dog properly. Many Staffords have made happy "relocations" from country life to the big city.

Staffordshire Bull Terriers can thrive in the big city as long as they are taken on frequent walks. Meeting friends in the park is a plus to city life.

kidneys and bladder. These stones, formed by crystals, cause the disease known as urolithiasis. Vets usually prescribe antibiotics to treat these infections.

A dog that develops a cataract will have cloudiness in the eye that can lead to blindness. Although surgery can help, the dog's sight cannot be restored to that of a normal dog. Annual checkups will help detect cataracts, and an affected dog should not be bred. Bilateral cataracts, also known as juvenile cataracts, occur in younger dogs, and are hereditary in the Stafford. The most commonly identified cataract is found in the posterior axial subcapsular region of the lens. Such cataracts mature as the dog grows older. In certain cases, the cataract can be detected in one eye before the other eye appears affected. In severe cases, the dog can go blind because of the intensity of the opacities.

Staffordshire Bull Terriers presently enjoy strong resistance to most orthopedic diseases, although there is concern in the

Provided they receive proper exercise, they can live comfortably in small apartments, though they are most content with plenty of room to run and play. City dwellers frequently visit the "dog parks" to allow their dogs the opportunity to run, though a leash is always necessary whenever your Stafford will be meeting strange dogs and people.

HEALTH CONSIDERATIONS IN THE STAFFORD

Unlike many breeds of pure-bred dog, the Staffordshire Bull Terrier is highly resistant to illness. The Staffordshire Bull Terrier does not suffer from susceptibility to many hereditary illnesses, though bilateral cataracts and kidney stones are reported, as are harelips and cleft palates in newborns. Cystine uroliths can affect a Stafford's

breed about hip dysplasia. Compared to other popular breeds, the Staffordshire's incidence of hip dysplasia is quite minimal. Responsible, ethical breeders screen their stock animals before including them in breeding programs. It's estimated that about one percent of the Staffordshire Bull Terrier population suffers from severe hip dysplasia, while about 20% test for some degree of dysplasia. In

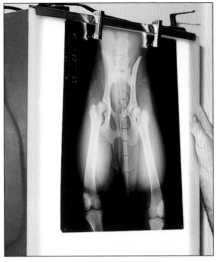

Although symptoms appear earlier, hip dysplasia can only be confirmed by a radiologist's evaluation of an x-ray once the dog has reached two years of age.

this 20%, most dogs will experience little, if any, discomfort, though it varies from dog to dog. Since hip dysplasia is a congenital illness, affected dogs should be bred so that the population is kept dysplasia-free. Other orthopedic concerns, even less serious than hip dysplasia, are elbow dysplasia and patellar luxation (affecting the kneecaps). Both the knees and the elbows can be screened for problems by x-ray, just as with the hips.

Staffordshire Bull Terriers prize the company of their owners, and it's easy to see why the feeling is mutual!

Breeders and vets warn new Staffordshire Bull Terrier owners to watch their dogs carefully. The breed has a very high pain threshold and can adjust to great discomfort without the owner realizing a problem. Staffords commonly succumb to joint and limb injuries, which can go unnoticed in many dogs.

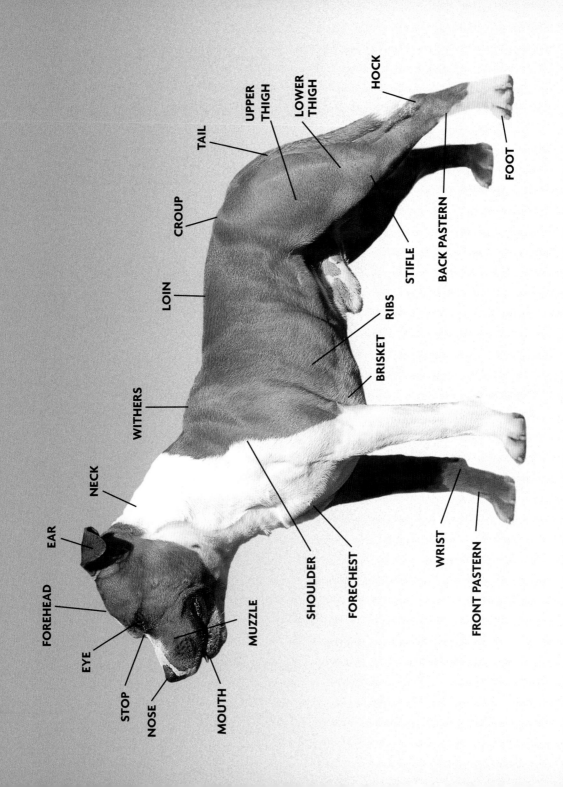

BREED STANDARD FOR THE

STAFFORDSHIRE BULL TERRIER

WHAT IS A STANDARD?

A breed standard is the official description of the way a dog should look and act. The standard is drafted by the parent club and then adopted by the American Kennel Club (AKC), the main national registering body for pure-bred dogs. It is the accepted "blueprint" by which breeders and judges evaluate the quality of Staffordshire Bull Terriers. Dogs shown in exhibition are compared to the breed standard. Only those dogs that "stack up" to the standard will earn the title of champion and therefore be deemed worthy of breeding.

While the standard is subject to the interpretation of the judge and breeder, it does attempt to emphasise the most important aspects of the dog. The Staffordshire Bull Terrier is first and foremost a strong, solid dog. The standard refers to musculature several times in describing the body and its parts.

The standard may vary from registry to registry and from country to country, although all breed standards attempt to describe essentially the same dog.

THE AKC STANDARD FOR THE STAFFORDSHIRE BULL TERRIER

General Appearance: The Staffordshire Bull Terrier is a smooth-coated dog. It should be of great strength for its size and, although muscular, should be active and agile.

Size, Proportion, Substance: Height at shoulder: 14 to 16 inches. Weight: Dogs, 28 to 38 pounds; bitches, 24 to 34 pounds,

Staffordshire Bull Terriers should appear muscular, active and agile, even when standing at attention.

Rose or half pricked-ears that are not large are desired in the Staffordshire Bull Terrier.

these heights being related to weights. Non-conformity with these limits is a fault. In proportion, the length of back, from withers to tail set, is equal to the distance from withers to ground.

Head: Short, deep through, broad skull, very pronounced cheek muscles, distinct stop, short foreface, black nose. Pink (Dudley) nose to be considered a serious fault. *Eyes*—Dark preferable, but may bear some relation to coat color. Round, of medium size, and set to look straight ahead. Light eyes or pink eye rims to be considered a fault, except that where the coat surrounding the eye is white the eye rim may be pink. *Ears*—Rose or half-pricked and not large. Full drop or full prick to be considered a serious fault. *Mouth*—A bite in which the outer side of the lower incisors touches the inner side of the upper incisors. The lips

All terriers are known for large teeth and strong jaws; this is especially so in the Staffordshire Bull Terrier.

should be tight and clean. The badly undershot or overshot bite is a serious fault.

Neck, Topline, Body: The neck is muscular, rather short, clean in outline and gradually widening toward the shoulders. The body is close coupled, with a level topline, wide front, deep brisket and well sprung ribs being rather light in the loins. The tail is undocked, of medium length, low set, tapering to a point and carried rather low. It should not curl much and may be likened to an old-fashioned pump handle. A tail that is too long or badly curled is a fault.

Forequarters: Legs straight and well boned, set rather far apart, without looseness at the shoulders and showing no weakness at the pasterns, from which point the feet turn out a little. Dewclaws on the forelegs may be removed. The feet should be well padded, strong and of medium size.

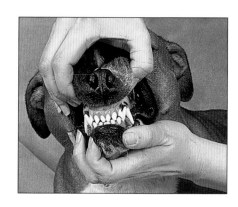

(Left) The Stafford's body should be close coupled with a level topline. (Right) A sleek brindle dog with a white blaze on his impressive broad chest.

Hindquarters: The hindquarters should be well muscled, hocks let down with stifles well bent. Legs should be parallel when viewed from behind. Dewclaws, if any, on the hind legs are generally removed. Feet as in front.

Coat: Smooth, short and close to the skin, not to be trimmed or dewhiskered.

Color: Red, fawn, white, black or blue, or any of these colors with white. Any shade of brindle or any shade of brindle with white. Black-and-tan or liver color to be disqualified.

Gait: Free, powerful and agile with economy of effort. Legs moving parallel when viewed from front or rear. Discernible drive from hind legs.

Temperament: From the past history of the Staffordshire Bull Terrier, the modern dog draws its character of indomitable courage, high intelligence, and tenacity. This, coupled with its affection for its friends, and children in particular, its off-duty quietness and trustworthy stability, makes it a foremost all-purpose dog.

Disqualification: Black-and-tan or liver color.

Approved November 14, 1989
Effective January 1, 1990

A Stafford with attractive red coloration. Judges do not place great importance on coloration, provided the dogs are not liver or black and tan.

EARS
Pricked ears are undesirable in the Stafford and considered a serious fault.

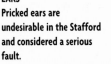

FOREFACE
The stop should be distinct and the foreface short. Lack of stop ruins the expression of the Staffordshire.

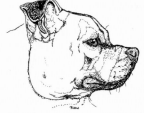

FOREQUARTERS
The legs should be straight and well boned, set well apart. The chest should be wide.

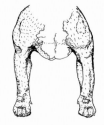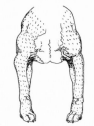

HINDQUARTERS
The hindlegs should be parallel when viewed from behind, never bowing in at the hocks.

TAIL
The desired tail is likened to an old-fashioned pump handle, never curled or carried high.

STAFFORDSHIRE BULL TERRIER

ARE YOU READY FOR THE STAFFORD?

The Staffordshire Bull Terrier offers the potential owner many advantages. This is a very easy-care dog: obedient, smooth-coated, intelligent and remarkably healthy. For an active dog owner who is willing to spend quality time with a dog, the Stafford is an excellent choice. The breed's dedication to home and family, its protective nature and its good-hearted spirit make the Stafford a king among canines. In the hands of a responsible owner, the Staffordshire Bull Terrier has few flaws.

The question remains: Are you that responsible owner? Make no mistake: you will be the beginning, middle and end of your Stafford's world. This is not a dog you can ignore. You will be his

The Staffordshire Bull Terrier is protective and devoted, making an alert guard dog for family and home.

favorite friend, walking companion, snoozing lap and dinner chum. Are you ready to "own" an unconditional best friend whom you raise from the tender age of eight weeks? Staffords abound in energy, more so than the average dog. They seek companionship and entertainment, and they love to entertain! An active, if not athletic, individual is the best

YOUR SCHEDULE . . .

If you lead an erratic, unpredictable life, with daily or weekly changes in your work requirements, consider the problems of owning a puppy. The new puppy has to be fed regularly, socialized (loved, petted, handled, introduced to other people) and, most importantly, allowed to go outdoors for house-training. As the dog gets older, he can be more tolerant of deviations in his feeding and relief schedule.

owner for a Stafford. Your Staffordshire Bull Terrier will enjoy an afternoon cycling or jogging on the beach, running beside you on horseback or playing chase in the garden. These kinds of activities keep the Stafford healthy in mind and body.

WHERE TO BEGIN?

If you are convinced that the Staffordshire Bull Terrier is the ideal dog for you, it's time to find where to find a puppy and what to look for. Locating a litter of Staffords should not present a problem for the new owner. You should inquire about breeders in your region who enjoy a good reputation in the breed. You are looking for an established breeder with outstanding dog ethics and a strong commitment to the breed. New owners should have as many questions as they have doubts. An established breeder is indeed the one to answer your four million questions and make you comfortable with your choice of the Staffordshire Bull Terrier. An established breeder will sell you a puppy at a fair price if, and only if, the breeder determines that you are a suitable, worthy owner of his/her dogs. An established breeder can be relied upon for advice, no matter what time of day or night. A reputable breeder will accept a puppy back, without questions, should you decide that this not the right dog for you.

When choosing a breeder, reputation is much more important than a convenient location. Owning a dog is not really a convenience, so convenience doesn't play a part like responsibility and commitment do. It's not convenient to have a four-legged wolf-creature crawling around your house, chewing, piddling and messing every room he enters. We don't choose to share our homes with dogs because it's convenient, but rather for the

TEMPERAMENT COUNTS

Your selection of a good puppy can be determined by your needs. A show potential or a good pet? It is your choice. Every puppy, however, should be of good temperament. Although show-quality puppies are bred and raised with emphasis on physical conformation, responsible breeders strive for equally good temperament. Do not buy from a breeder who concentrates solely on physical beauty at the expense of personality.

companionship and other benefits of this thing we call dog owner- ship. The local novice breeder, trying so hard to get rid of that first litter of ten puppies, is more than accommodating and anxious to sell you one. That breeder lives only a couple of miles away, but will charge you as much as any established breeder. The novice breeder isn't going to interrogate you and your family about your intentions with the puppy, the environment and training you can provide, etc. That breeder will be nowhere to be found when your poorly bred, badly adjusted four- pawed monster starts to growl and spit up at midnight or eat the family cat!

While health considerations in the Stafford are not nearly as daunting as in most other breeds, socialization is a breeder concern of immense importance. Since the Stafford has a natural aggressive nature towards other dogs, socializa- tion is

While color should not be a major factor is selecting a puppy, signs of good health and sound tempera- ment must play key roles in your choice.

the first and best way to prevent this instinct from developing into a problem. Good breeders intro- duce their puppies to other dogs at an early age to promote their acceptance of fellow canines. A good way to assess your pup's potential temperament is to meet one or both of the parents. If they are aggressive, you may have a future problem with the pup.

CHOOSING A BREEDER

Choosing a breeder is an impor- tant first step in dog ownership. Fortunately, the majority of Staffordshire Bull Terrier breeders are devoted to the breed and its well-being. New owners should have little problem finding a reputable breeder in their part of the country. The American Kennel Club and the national parent club for the breed, the Staffordshire Bull Terrier Club, Inc., are reliable sources of ethical breeders. Potential owners are encouraged to attend a dog show to see the

A HEALTHY PUP

You should not even think about buying a puppy that looks sick, under- nourished, overly frightened or nervous. Sometimes a timid puppy will warm up to you after a 30-minute "let's-get-acquainted" session.

ARE YOU A FIT OWNER?
If the breeder from whom you are buying a puppy asks you a lot of personal questions, do not be insulted. Such a breeder wants to be sure that you will be a fit provider for his puppy.

Choose a pup with a sweet personality that wants to get close to you. A well-socialized Stafford puppy thrives on the company of humans.

Staffords in action, to meet the breeders and handlers firsthand and to get an idea what Staffords look like outside of a photographer's lens. Provided you approach the handlers when they are not engaged in grooming or handling the dogs, most are more than willing to answer questions, recommend breeders and give advice.

Once you have contacted and met a breeder or two and made your choice about which breeder is best suited to your needs, it's time to visit the litter. Keep in mind that many top breeders have waiting lists. Sometimes new owners have to wait a year or more for a puppy. If you are really committed to the breeder whom you've selected, then you will wait (and hope for an early arrival!). If not, you may have to go with your second- or third-choice breeder. Don't be too

anxious, however. If the breeder doesn't have any waiting list, or any customers, there is probably a good reason. It's no different than visiting a restaurant with no clientele. The better establishments always have waiting lists—and it's usually worth the wait. Besides, isn't a puppy more important than a fancy dinner?

Stafford puppies can be feisty and a bit quarrelsome, but the new owner should never select the puppy who appears to be a mean-spirited instigator. A sweet-natured puppy with an outgoing personality is the new owner's

best choice. When viewing a litter of Stafford puppies, you are looking for friendly, bright-eyed pups. Hopefully that describes the whole litter, although there is usually one shy pup who cannot compete with the rest. Breeders commonly allow visitors to see the litter by around the fifth or sixth week, and puppies leave for their new homes between the eighth and tenth week. Breeders who permit their puppies to leave early are more interested in making a profit than in their puppies' welll-being. Puppies need to learn the rules of the trade from their dams, and most dams continue teaching the pups manners and dos and don'ts until around the eighth week. Breeders spend significant amounts of time with the Stafford toddlers so that they are able to interact with the "other species," i.e., humans! Staffords get along with humans, but other canines concern them. Given the long history that dogs and humans have, bonding between the two species is natural but must be nurtured. A well-bred, well-socialized Staffordshire Bull Terrier pup wants nothing more than to be near you and please you. That's as convenient as a puppy can be!

What other considerations might an owner entertain in choosing a pup? Most breeders agree that the sex of the puppy is immaterial. Staffords usually

TIME TO GO HOME

Breeders rarely release puppies until they are eight to ten weeks of age. This is an acceptable age for most breeds of dog, excepting Toy breeds, which are not released until around 12 weeks, given their petite sizes. If a breeder has a puppy that is 12 weeks of age or older, he is likely well socialized and house-trained. Be sure that he is otherwise healthy before deciding to take him home.

An athlete at heart, the Stafford has strong legs to match his strong jaws. An active person with time to exercise the dog is the best owner for the Stafford.

friendly, and has a compact and cobby body with a strong head, well in balance with the body, you will have a quality Staffordshire Bull Terrier.

COMMITMENT OF OWNERSHIP
After considering all of these factors, you have most likely

cannot cohabitate in same-sex pairs, so owners considering a pair must get a male and a female.

Coloration is probably the most common preference among new owners. Certainly some handsome Stafford in this book has caught the reader's eye and convinced him of one color over another. Breeders do not place much importance on color, although liver and black and tan are strictly prohibited from the show ring. This seemingly random prejudice stems from interbreeding of the Stafford with some liver and black and tan breeds in the past. Today such crosses are frowned upon. Regardless of which color the new owner favors, dark pigment on the nose and paw pads is important. Of course, the temperament and structure of the puppy must be considered before color. As long as the puppy is outgoing and

PEDIGREE VS. REGISTRATION CERTIFICATE

Too often new owners are confused between these two important documents. Your puppy's pedigree, essentially a family tree, is a written record of a dog's genealogy of three generations or more. The pedigree will show you the names as well as performance titles of all dogs in your pup's background. Your breeder must provide you with a registration application, with his part properly filled out. You must complete the application and send it to the AKC with the proper fee. Every puppy must come from a litter that has been AKC-registered by the breeder, born in the USA and from a sire and dam that are also registered with the AKC.

The seller must provide you with complete records to identify the puppy. The AKC requires that the seller provide the buyer with the following: breed; sex, color and markings; date of birth; litter number (when available); names and registration numbers of the parents; breeder's name; and date sold or delivered.

already made some very important decisions about selecting your puppy. You have chosen the Staffordshire Bull Terrier, which means that you have decided which characteristics you want in a dog and what type of dog will best fit into your family and lifestyle. If you have selected a breeder, you have gone a step further—you have done your research and found a responsible, conscientious person who breeds quality Staffords and who should be a reliable source of help as you and your puppy adjust to life together. If you have observed a litter in action, you have obtained a firsthand look at the dynamics of a puppy "pack" and, thus, you have gotten to learn about each pup's individual personality—perhaps you have even found one that particularly appeals to you.

However, even if you have not yet found the Staffordshire Bull Terrier puppy of your dreams, observing pups will help you learn to recognize certain behavior and to determine what a pup's behavior indicates about his temperament. You will be able to pick out which pups are the leaders, which ones are less outgoing, which ones are confident, which ones are shy, playful, friendly, aggressive, etc. Equally as important, you will learn to recognize what a healthy pup should look and act like. All of these things will help you in your search, and

When you buy a Stafford puppy, you are entering into a commitment for at least the next decade, likely longer. Don't make the decision to own a Stafford too hastily.

when you find the Staffordshire Bull Terrier that was meant for you, you will know it!

Researching your breed, selecting a responsible breeder and observing as many pups as possible are all important steps on the way to dog ownership. It may seem like a lot of effort...and you have not even brought the pup home yet! Remember, though, you cannot be too careful when it comes to deciding on the type of dog you want and finding out about your prospective pup's background. Buying a puppy is not—or *should* not be—just another whimsical purchase. This is one instance in which you actually do get to choose your own

family! You may be thinking that buying a puppy should be fun—it should not be so serious and so much work. Keep in mind that your puppy is not a cuddly stuffed toy or decorative lawn ornament, but a creature who will become a real member of your family, and you will realize that while buying a puppy is a pleasurable and exciting endeavor, it is not something to be taken lightly. Relax...the fun will start when the pup comes home!

Always keep in mind that a puppy is nothing more than a baby in a furry disguise...a baby who is virtually helpless in a human world and who trusts his owner for fulfillment of his basic needs for survival. In addition to

food, water and shelter, your pup needs care, protection, guidance and love. If you are not prepared to commit to this, then you are not prepared to own a dog.

"Wait a minute," you say. "How hard could this be? All of my neighbors own dogs and they seem to be doing just fine. Why should I have to worry about all of this?" Well, you should not worry about it; in fact, you will probably find that once your Staffordshire Bull Terrier pup gets used to his new home, he will fall into his place in the family quite naturally. But it never hurts to emphasize the commitment of dog ownership. With some time and patience, it is really not too difficult to raise a curious and exuberant Stafford pup to be a well-adjusted and well-mannered adult dog—a dog that could be your most loyal friend.

IN DUE TIME
It will take at least two weeks for your puppy to become accustomed to his new surroundings. Give him lots of love, attention, handling, frequent opportunities to relieve himself, a diet he likes to eat and a place he can call his own.

PREPARING PUPPY'S PLACE IN YOUR HOME

Researching your breed and finding a breeder are only two aspects of the "homework" you will have to do before bringing your Stafford puppy home. You will also have to prepare your home and family for the new addition. Much like you would prepare a nursery for a newborn baby, you will need to designate a place in your home that will be the puppy's own. How you prepare your home will depend on how much freedom the dog will be allowed. Will he be confined to one room or a specific

area in the house, or will he be allowed to roam as he pleases? Will he spend most of his time in the house or will he be primarily an outdoor dog? Whatever you decide, you must ensure that he has a place that he can call his own.

When you bring your new puppy into your home, you are bringing him into what will become his home as well. Obviously, you did not buy a puppy so that he could take control of your house, but in order for a puppy to grow into a stable, well-adjusted dog, he has to feel comfortable in his surroundings. Remember, he is leaving the warmth and security of his mother and littermates, as well as the familiarity of the only place he has ever known, so it is important to make his transition as easy as possible. By preparing a place

These Stafford puppies are enjoying a photo opportunity in a strange environment.

Breeders often allow families into the whelping area to meet their puppies. Giving the puppies as much exposure to different experiences is key to the socialization process.

in your home for the puppy, you are making him feel as welcome as possible in a strange new place. It should not take him long to get used to it, but the sudden shock of being transplanted is somewhat traumatic for a young pup. Imagine how a small child would feel in the same situation—that is how your puppy must be feeling. It is up to you to reassure him and to let him know, "Little fellow, you are going to like it here!"

WHAT YOU SHOULD BUY

CRATE

To someone unfamiliar with the use of crates in dog training, it may seem like punishment to shut a dog in a crate. However, this is not the case at all. Crates are not cruel—crates have many humane and highly effective uses in dog care and training. For example, crate training is a very popular and very successful housebreaking method, a crate can keep your dog safe during travel and, perhaps most importantly, a crate provides your dog with a place of

PHOTO COURTESY OF DOSKOCIL

his own in your home. It serves as a "doggie bedroom" of sorts—your Stafford can curl up in his crate when he wants to sleep or when he just needs a break. Many dogs sleep in their crates overnight. When lined with soft blankets and with his favorite toy inside, a crate becomes a cozy pseudo-den for your dog. Like his ancestors, he too will seek out the comfort and retreat of a den—you just happen to be providing him with something a little more luxurious than leaves and twigs lining a dirty ditch.

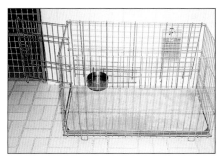

Your Stafford will welcome a place of his own for safety and retreat.

As far as purchasing a crate, the type that you buy is up to you. It will most likely be one of the two most popular types: wire or fiberglass. There are advantages and disadvantages to each type. For example, a wire crate is more open, allowing the air to flow through and affording the dog a view of what is going on around him, while a fiberglass crate is sturdier. Both can double as travel crates, providing protection for the dog in the car.

The size of the crate is another thing to consider. Puppies do not stay puppies forever—in fact, sometimes it seems as if they grow right before your eyes. A small crate may be fine for a very young Stafford pup, but it will not do him much good for long! Unless you have the money and the inclination to buy a new crate every time your pup has a growth

spurt, it is better to get one that will accommodate your dog both as a pup and at full size. A medium- to large-size crate will be necessary for a full-grown Stafford; keep the eventual height of 14–16 inches at the shoulder in mind, allowing for enough room for the dog to stand and lie down.

BEDDING

A blanket or crate pad in the dog's crate will help the dog feel more at home. First, these things will take the place of the leaves, twigs, etc., that the pup would use in the wild to make a den; the pup can make his own "burrow" in the

The most valuable accessory you can buy for your Stafford is a crate. It will become an essential tool in training and providing safety for your dog.

CRATE-TRAINING TIPS

During crate training, you should partition off the section of the crate in which the pup stays. If he is given too big an area, this will hinder your training efforts. Crate training is based on the fact that a dog does not like to soil his sleeping quarters, so it is ineffective to keep a pup in an area that is so big that he can eliminate in one end and get far enough away from it to sleep. Also, you want to make the crate den-like for the pup. Blankets and a favorite toy will make the crate cozy for the small pup; as he grows, you may want to evict some of his "roommates" to make more room. It will take some coaxing at first, but be patient. Given some time to get used to it, your pup will adapt to his new home-within-a-home quite nicely.

crate. Although your pup is far removed from his den-making ancestors, the denning instinct is still a part of his genetic makeup. Second, until you bring your pup home, he has been sleeping amid the warmth of his mother and littermates, and while a blanket is not the same as a warm, breathing body, it still provides heat and something with which to snuggle. You will want to wash your pup's bedding frequently in case he has a potty accident in his crate, and replace or remove any blanket or padding that becomes ragged and starts to fall apart.

Toys

Toys are a must for dogs of all ages, especially for curious playful pups. Puppies are the "children" of the dog world, and what child does not love toys? Chew toys provide enjoyment to both dog and owner—your dog will enjoy playing with his favorite toys, while you will enjoy the fact that they distract him from your

PUPPY PROBLEMS
The majority of problems that are commonly seen in young pups will disappear as your Stafford gets older. However, how you deal with problems when he is young will determine how he reacts to discipline as an adult dog. It is important to establish who is boss (ideally it will be you!) right away when you are first bonding with your dog. This bond will set the tone for the rest of your life together.

expensive shoes and leather sofa. Puppies love to chew; in fact, chewing is a physical need for pups as they are teething, and everything looks appetizing! The full range of your possessions—from old dishrag to Oriental rug—are fair game in the eyes of a teething pup. Puppies are not all that discerning when it comes to finding something to literally "sink their teeth into"—everything tastes great!

Stafford puppies are fairly aggressive chewers with strong jaws, so only the hardest, strongest toys should be offered to them. Breeders advise owners to resist stuffed toys, because they can become de-stuffed in no time.

Tire swing or extra-large chew toy? The playful and innovative Stafford puppy will find plenty of ways to amuse himself.

The overly excited pup may ingest the stuffing, which is neither nutritious nor digestible.

Similarly, squeaky toys are quite popular, but must be avoided for the Stafford. Perhaps a squeaky toy can be used as an aid in training, but not for free play. If a pup "disembowels" one of these, the small plastic squeaker inside can be dangerous if swallowed. Monitor the condition of all your pup's toys carefully and get rid of any that have been chewed to the point of becoming potentially dangerous.

Be careful of natural bones, which have a tendency to splinter

TOYS, TOYS, TOYS!

With a big variety of dog toys available, and so many that look like they would be a lot of fun for a dog, be careful in your selection. It is amazing what a set of puppy teeth can do to an innocent-looking toy, so, obviously, safety is a major consideration. Be sure to choose the most durable products that you can find. Hard nylon bones and toys are a safe bet, and many of them are offered in different scents and flavors that will be sure to capture your Stafford's attention. It is always fun to play a game of fetch with your dog, and there are balls and flying discs that are specially made to withstand dog teeth.

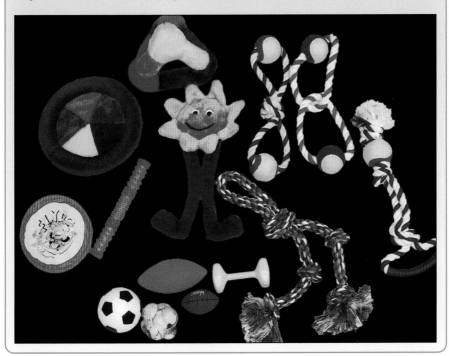

The Stafford's strength is evident just by looking at him! Therefore, it is important to purchase only leashes and collars made of the most durable materials for your Staffordshire Bull Terrier.

into sharp, dangerous pieces. Also be careful of rawhide, which can turn into pieces that are easy to swallow or into a mushy mess on your carpet.

LEASH

Many owners like to "dress up" their Staffords with ornamental collars.

A nylon leash is probably the best option, as it is the most resistant to puppy teeth should your pup take a liking to chewing on his leash. Of course, this is a habit that should be nipped in the bud, but, if your pup likes to chew on his leash, he has a very slim chance of being able to chew through the strong nylon. Nylon leashes are also lightweight, which is good for a young Stafford puppy who is just getting used to the idea of walking on a leash. For everyday walking and safety purposes, the nylon leash is a good choice.

As your pup grows up and gets used to walking on the leash,

and only if he can do it politely, you may want to purchase a flexible leash, which allows you to extend the length to give the dog a broader area to explore or to pull in the leash when you want to keep him close. Of course there are special leashes for training purposes, as well as harnesses for Staffords that tend to pull while walking. Some owners prefer the harness to the leash and collar. As your Stafford pup grows into his muscles, you will need to purchase a thicker leash.

COLLAR

Your pup should get used to wearing a collar all the time since you will want to attach his ID tags to it. Also, you have to attach the

Unfortunately, when a puppy is bought by someone who does not take into consideration the time and attention that dog ownership requires, it is the puppy who suffers when he is either abandoned or placed in a shelter by a frustrated owner. So all of the "homework" you do in preparation for your pup's arrival will benefit you both. The more informed you are, the more you will know what to expect and the better equipped you will be to handle the ups and downs of raising a puppy. Hopefully, everyone in the household is willing to do his part in raising and caring for the pup. The anticipation of owning a dog often brings a lot of promises from excited family members: "I will walk him every day," "I will feed him," "I will house-train him," etc., but these things take time and effort, and promises can easily be forgotten once the novelty of the new pet has worn off.

leash to something! A lightweight nylon collar is a good choice; make sure that it fits snugly enough so that the pup cannot wriggle out of it, but is loose enough so that it will not be uncomfortably tight around the pup's neck. You should be able to fit a finger between the pup and the collar. It may take some time for your pup to get used to wearing the collar, but soon he will not even notice that it is there. Choke collars are to be used *only* for

training and *only* by an owner who knows exactly how to use it. When you change to a stronger leather or thicker nylon leash to walk your Stafford, you will need a stronger collar as well.

FOOD AND WATER BOWLS
Your pup will need two bowls, one for food and one for water. You may want two sets of bowls, one for inside and one for outside, depending on where the dog will be fed and where he will be spending time. Stainless steel or sturdy plastic bowls are popular choices, but plastic bowls tend to be more chewable. Dogs tend not to chew on the steel variety, which can be sterilized. It is important to buy sturdy bowls since anything is in danger of being chewed by puppy teeth and you do not want your dog to be

Accustom the puppy to the collar at a young age. Buckle collars are acceptable for young puppies. Identification tags can be attached to the buckle collar.

Your pet shop should carry a full range of food and water bowls. Choose durable, easily cleaned bowls for your Stafford.

PHOTO COURTESY OF MIKKI PET PRODUCTS.

constantly chewing apart his bowl (for his safety and for your wallet!).

CLEANING SUPPLIES
Until a pup is house-trained, you will be doing a lot of cleaning. Potty accidents will occur, which is okay in the beginning because he does not know any better. All you can do is clean up any accidents. Old rags, towels, newspapers and a safe disinfectant are good to have on hand.

BEYOND THE BASICS
The items previously discussed are the bare necessities. You will find out what else you need as you go along—grooming supplies, flea/tick protection, baby gates to partition a room, etc. These things will vary depending on your situation, but it is important that you have everything you need to feed and make your Staffordshire Bull Terrier comfortable in his first few days at home.

PUPPY-PROOFING YOUR HOME
Aside from making sure that your Stafford will be comfortable in your home, you also have to make sure that your home is safe for your Stafford. This means taking precautions that your pup will not get into anything he should not get into and that there is nothing within his reach that may harm him should he sniff it, chew it, inspect it, etc. This probably

seems obvious since, while you are primarily concerned with your pup's safety, at the same time you do not want your belongings to be ruined.

Breakables should be placed out of reach if your dog is to have full run of the house. If he is to be limited to certain places within the house, keep any potentially dangerous items in the "off-limits" areas. An electrical cord can pose a danger should the puppy decide to taste it—and who is going to convince a pup that it would not make a great chew toy? Cords should be fastened tightly against the wall, out of puppy's sight and reach. If your dog is going to spend time in a crate, make sure that there is nothing near his crate that he can reach if he sticks his curious little nose or paws through the openings. Just as you would with a child, keep all household cleaners and chemicals where he cannot get to them. Be careful in the garage, too; antifreeze is especially toxic to dogs.

It is also important to make sure that the outside of your home is safe. Of course your puppy should never be unsupervised, but a pup let loose in the yard will want to run and explore, and he should be granted that freedom. Do not let a fence give you a false sense of security; you would be surprised how crafty (and persistent) a dog can be in figuring out

PUPPY FEEDING
You will probably start feeding your Stafford pup the same food that he has been getting from the breeder; the breeder should give you a few days' supply to start you off. Although you should not give your pup too many treats, you will want to have puppy treats on hand for coaxing, training, rewards, etc. Be careful, though, as a small pup's calorie requirements are relatively low and a few treats can add up to almost a full day's worth of calories without the required nutrition.

how to dig under and squeeze his way through small holes, or to jump or climb over a fence. The remedy is to make the fence high enough so that it really is impossible for your dog to get over it (about 6 feet should suffice), and well embedded into the ground. Be sure to secure any gaps in the fence. Check the fence periodically to ensure that it is in good

Be certain to have your new puppy checked by your vet as soon as possible after picking him up from the breeder.

shape and make repairs as needed; a very determined pup may return to the same spot to "work on it" until he is able to get through.

FIRST TRIP TO THE VET

You have picked out your puppy, and your home and family are ready. Now all you have to do is pick up your Stafford from the breeder and the fun begins, right? Well…not so fast. Something else you need to prepare is your pup's first trip to the veterinarian. Perhaps the breeder can recommend someone in the area that specializes in bull and terrier breeds, or maybe you know some other Stafford owners who can

suggest a good vet. Either way, you should have an appointment arranged for your pup before you pick him up and plan on taking him for a checkup before bringing him home.

The pup's first visit will consist of an overall examination to make sure that the pup does not have any problems that are not apparent to you. The veterinarian will also set up a schedule for the pup's vaccinations; the breeder will inform you of which ones the pup has already received and the vet can continue from there.

INTRODUCTION TO THE FAMILY

Everyone in the house will be excited about the puppy's coming home and will want to pet him and play with him, but it is best

PET INSURANCE

Just like you can insure your car, your house and your own health, you likewise can insure your dog's health. Investigate a pet insurance policy by talking to your vet. Depending on the age of your dog, the breed and the kind of coverage you desire, your policy can be very affordable. Most policies cover accidental injuries, poisoning and thousands of medical problems and illnesses, including cancers. Some carriers also offer routine care and immunization coverage.

to make the intro-
ductions low-key
so as not to over-
whelm the puppy.
He is apprehensive
already. It is the
first time he has
been separated
from his mother
and the breeder,
and the ride to
your home is likely
the first time he
has been in a car.
The last thing you
want to do is
smother him, as
this will only
frighten him
further. This is not
to say that human
contact is not
extremely neces-
sary at this stage,
because this is the
time when a
connection
between the pup
and his human
family is formed.
Gentle petting and
soothing words
should help console him, as well
as just putting him down and
letting him explore on his own
(under your watchful eye, of
course).

Be aware of the pup's growth and adjust his collar regularly. It will seem that the puppy is growing on a daily basis!

The pup may approach the
family members or may busy
himself with exploring for awhile.
Gradually, each person should
spend some time with the pup,
one at a time, crouching down to
get as close to the pup's level as
possible while letting him sniff
their hands and petting him
gently. He definitely needs human
attention and he needs to be
touched—this is how to form an
immediate bond. Just remember

that the pup is experiencing a lot of things for the first time, at the same time. There are new people, new noises, new smells and new things to investigate, so be gentle, be affectionate and be as comforting as you can be.

YOUR PUP'S FIRST NIGHT HOME

You have traveled home with your new pup safely in his crate or on a passenger's lap. He's been to the vet for a thorough checkup; he's been weighed, his papers examined; perhaps he's even been vaccinated and wormed as well. He's met the whole family, including the excited children and the less-than-happy cat. He's explored his area, his new bed, the yard and anywhere else he's been permitted. He's eaten his first meal at home and relieved himself in the proper place. He's heard lots of new sounds, smelled new friends and seen more of the outside world than ever before. That was the just the first day! He's exhausted and is ready for bed…or so you think!

It's puppy's first night and you are ready to say "Good night"— keep in mind that this is puppy's first night ever to be sleeping alone. His dam and littermates are no longer at paw's length and he's a bit scared, cold and lonely. Be reassuring to your new family member, but this is not the time to spoil him and give in to his

NATURAL TOXINS
Examine your grass and landscaping before bringing your puppy home. Many varieties of plants have leaves, stems or flowers that are toxic if ingested, and you can depend on a curious puppy to investigate them. Ask your vet for information on poisonous plants or research them at your library.

If you see your dog carrying a piece of vegetation in his mouth, approach him in a quiet, disinterested manner, avoid eye contact, pet him and gradually remove the plant from his mouth. Alternatively, offer him a treat and maybe he'll drop the plant on his own accord. Be sure no toxic plants are growing in your own yard or kept in your home.

inevitable whining.

Puppies whine. They whine to let others know where they are and hopefully to get company out of it. Place your pup in his new bed or crate in his room and close the door. Mercifully, he may fall asleep without a peep. If the inevitable occurs, ignore the whining; he is fine. Be strong and keep his interest in mind. Do not allow your heart to become guilty and visit the pup. He will fall asleep eventually.

Many breeders recommend placing a piece of bedding from the pup's former home in his new bed so that he recognizes the scent of his littermates. Others still advise placing a hot water bottle in his bed for warmth. This latter may be a good idea provided the pup doesn't attempt to suckle—he'll get good and wet and may not fall asleep so fast.

Puppy's first night can be

THE RIDE HOME

Taking your dog from the breeder to your home in a car can be a very uncomfortable experience for both of you. The puppy will have been taken from his warm, friendly, safe environment and brought into a strange new environment—an environment that moves! Be prepared for loose bowels, urination, crying, whining and even fear biting. With proper love and encouragement when you arrive home, the stress of the trip should quickly disappear.

somewhat stressful for the pup and his new family. Remember that you are setting the tone of nighttime at your house. Unless you want to play with your pup every night at 10 p.m., midnight and 2 a.m., don't initiate the habit. Your family will thank you, and soon so will your pup!

PREVENTING PUPPY PROBLEMS

SOCIALIZATION

Now that you have done all of the preparatory work and have helped your pup get accustomed to his new home and family, it is about time for you to have some fun! Socializing your Staffordshire Bull Terrier pup gives you the opportunity to show off your new friend, and your pup gets to reap the benefits of being an adorable

Puppies require attention and instruction. The first few days in your home should be completely under control. Do not overwhelm the puppy with too many new experiences and people all at once.

creature that people will coo over, want to pet and, in general, think is absolutely precious!

Besides getting to know his new family, your puppy should be exposed to other people, animals and situations. This will help him become well adjusted as he grows up and less prone to being timid or fearful of the new things he will encounter. Your pup's socialization began at the breeder's, but now it is your responsibility to continue it. The socialization he receives up until the age of 12 weeks is the most critical, as this is the time when he forms his impressions of the outside world. Be especially careful during the eight-to-ten-week-old period, also known as the fear period. The interaction he receives during this time should be gentle and reassuring. Lack of socialization can

manifest itself in fear and aggression as the dog grows up. He needs lots of human contact, affection, handling and exposure to other animals, although he should not be exposed to dogs you don't know well until he has been properly immunized.

Once your pup has received his necessary vaccinations, feel free to take him out and about (on his leash, of course). Take him around the neighborhood, take him on your daily errands, let people pet him, let him meet other dogs and pets, etc. Puppies do not have to try to make friends; there will be no shortage of people who will want to introduce themselves. Just make sure

THE COCOA WARS

Chocolate contains the chemical thebromine, which is poisonous to dogs, although "chocolates" especially made for dogs are safe (as they don't actually contain chocolate) but not recommended. Any item that encourages your dog to enjoy the taste of cocoa should be discouraged. You should also exercise caution when using mulch in your yard or garden. This frequently contains cocoa hulls, and dogs have been known to die from eating the mulch.

Consistency in Training

Dogs, being pack animals, naturally need a leader, or else they try to establish dominance in their packs. When you bring a dog into your family, the choice of who becomes the leader and who becomes the pack is entirely up to you! Your pup's intuitive quest for dominance, coupled with the fact that it is nearly impossible to look at an adorable Stafford pup with his "puppy-dog" eyes and not cave in, give the pup almost an unfair advantage in getting the upper hand!

A pup will definitely test the waters to see what he can and cannot do. Do not give in to those pleading eyes—stand your ground when it comes to disciplining the pup and make sure that all family members do the same. It will only confuse the pup when mom tells him to get off the couch when he is used to sitting up there with Dad to watch the nightly news.

Staffordshire Bull Terrier puppies learn about the world through their association with their dam and littermates. Breeders allow pups to be handled by people to further the pup's socialization.

that you carefully supervise each meeting. If the neighborhood children want to say hello, for example, that is great—children and Staffords usually become fast friends. However, sometimes an excited child can unintentionally handle a pup too roughly or an overzealous pup can playfully nip a little too hard. You want to make socialization experiences positive ones. What a pup learns during this very formative stage will impact his attitude toward future encounters. You want your dog to be comfortable around everyone. A pup that has a bad experience with a child may grow up to be a dog that is shy around or aggressive toward children.

PUP MEETS WORLD

Thorough socialization includes not only meeting new people but also being introduced to new experiences such as riding in the car, having his coat brushed, hearing the television, walking in a crowd—the list is endless. The more your pup experiences, and the more positive the experiences are, the less of a shock and the less frightening it will be for your pup to encounter new things.

Providing playthings, like safe chew toys, from an early age helps channel the pups' chewing instincts in positive ways.

Avoid discrepancies by having all members of the household decide on the rules before the pup even comes home…and be consistent in enforcing them! Early training shapes the dog's personality, so you cannot be unclear in what you expect.

COMMON PUPPY PROBLEMS

The best way to prevent problems is to be proactive in stopping an undesirable behavior as soon as it starts. The old saying "You can't teach an old dog new tricks" does not necessarily hold true, but it *is* true that it is much easier to discourage bad behavior in a young developing pup than to wait until the pup's bad behavior becomes the adult dog's bad habit. There are some problems that are especially prevalent in puppies as they develop.

NIPPING

As puppies start to teethe, they feel the need to sink their teeth into anything available…unfortunately that includes your fingers, arms, hair, and toes. You may find this behavior cute for the first five seconds…until you feel just how sharp those puppy teeth are. This is something you want to discourage immediately and consistently with a firm "No!" (or whatever number of firm "Nos" it takes for him to understand that you mean business). Then replace your finger with an appropriate chew toy. While this behavior is merely annoying when the dog is young, it can become dangerous as your Stafford's adult teeth grow in and his jaws develop if he continues to think it is okay nip at and nibble on his friends. You do not want to take a chance with a Stafford, as this is a breed whose jaws become very strong. Your pup does not mean any harm with a friendly nip, but he also does not know his own strength.

CRYING/WHINING

Your pup will often cry, whine, whimper, howl or make some

PROBLEM CHILD?

Training your puppy takes much patience and can be frustrating at times, but you should see results from your efforts. If you have a puppy that seems untrainable, take him to a trainer or behaviorist. The dog may have a personality problem that requires the help of a professional, or perhaps you need help in learning how to train your dog.

type of commotion when he is left alone. This is basically his way of calling out for attention to make sure that you know he is there and that you have not forgotten about him. He feels insecure when he is left alone, when you are out of the house and he is in his crate or when you are in another part of the house and he cannot see you. The noise he is making is an expression of the anxiety he feels at being alone, so he needs to be taught that being alone is okay. You are not actually training the dog to stop making noise, you are training him to feel comfortable when he is alone and thus removing the need for him to make the noise.

This is where the crate with a cozy blanket and his favorite toy comes in handy. You want to know that he is safe when you are not there to supervise, and you

Leaving the security and familiarity of his canine family is a big change for the pup that requires your sensitivity.

know that he will be safe in his crate rather than roaming freely about the house. In order for the pup to stay in his crate without making a fuss, he needs to be comfortable in his crate. On that note, it is extremely important that the crate is never used as a form of punishment, or the pup will develop a negative association with the crate.

Accustom the pup to the crate in short, gradually increasing time intervals in which you put him in the crate, maybe with a treat, and stay in the room with him. If he cries or makes a fuss, do not go to him, but stay in his sight. Gradually he will realize that staying in his crate is just fine without your help, and it will not be so traumatic for him when you are not around. You may want to leave the radio on softly when you leave the house; the sound of human voices may be comforting to him.

It is very important that all family members and everyone who meets your new puppy handle him with care.

Your Staffordshire Bull Terrier looks up to you, his loving owner, to provide for all aspects of his care and well-being.

STAFFORDSHIRE BULL TERRIER

DIETARY AND FEEDING CONSIDERATIONS

You have probably heard it a thousand times, "you are what you eat." Believe it or not, it's very true. Dogs are what you feed them because they have little

Staffordshire Bull Terrier puppies get the best start in life by nursing from their mothers.

FOOD PREFERENCE

Selecting the best dry dog food is difficult. There is no majority consensus among veterinary scientists as to the value of nutrient analysis (protein, fat, fiber, moisture, ash, cholesterol, minerals, etc.). All agree that feeding trials are what matter most, but you also have to consider the individual dog. The dog's weight, age and activity level, and what pleases his taste, all must be considered. It is probably best to take the advice of your veterinarian. Every dog has individual dietary requirements, and should be fed accordingly.

If your dog is fed a good dry food, he does not require supplements of meat or vegetables. Dogs do appreciate a little variety in their diets, so you may choose to stay with the same brand but vary the flavor. Alternatively, you may wish to add a little flavored stock to give a difference to the taste.

choice in the matter. Even those people who truly want to feed their dogs the best can be confused about how to do so. With such a wide range of complete foods now available, only knowing what is best for your dog will help you make an informed decision and enable you to provide him with balanced nutrition.

Dog foods are produced in three basic types: dry, semi-moist and canned. Dry foods are helpful for the cost-conscious because they are much less expensive than semi-moist and canned. Dry foods contain the least fat and the most preservatives. Most canned foods are 60 to 70% water, while semi-moist foods are so full of sugar that they are the least preferred by owners, though dogs welcome them (as a child does candy).

Stafford puppy diets should be balanced for your puppy's needs. Supplementation, unless advised, can actually be harmful to a growing pup.

Three stages of development must be considered when selecting a diet for your dog: the puppy stage, the adult stage and the senior stage.

PUPPY STAGE

Puppies have a natural instinct to suck milk from their mother's nipples. They should exhibit this behavior from the first day of their lives. If they don't suckle within a few hours, the breeder should attempt to put them onto their dam's nipples to feed, selecting ones with plenty of milk. If they still fail to feed, the breeder will have to feed them himself under the advice and guidance of a veterinarian. This will involve a baby bottle and a special formula. Despite there being some excellent formulas available, their dam's milk is best because it contains colostrum, a sort of antibiotic milk that protects the puppy during the first eight to ten weeks of their lives.

Puppies should be allowed to nurse for about the first six weeks.

Starting around the third or fourth week, the breeder will begin to introduce small portions of suitable solid food. Most breeders like to introduce alternate milk and meat meals initially, building up to weaning time.

By the time they are seven or a maximum of eight weeks old, the puppies should be completely weaned and fed solely a proprietary puppy food. During this period, selection of the diet is most important, as puppies grow fastest during their first year of life. Growth foods can be recommended by your vet or breeder, and young dogs can be kept on this diet for up to 18 months.

Puppy diets should be balanced for your dog's needs, and supplements of vitamins, minerals and protein should not be necessary.

ADULT DIETS

A dog is considered an adult when he has stopped growing in height and/or length. Do not consider the dog's weight when the decision is made to switch from a puppy diet to an adult-

STORING DOG FOOD

You must store your dry dog food carefully. Open packages of dog food quickly lose their vitamin value, usually within 90 days of being opened. Mold spores and vermin could also contaminate the food.

maintenance diet. Again you should rely upon your vet or breeder to recommend an acceptable maintenance diet. Major dog-food manufacturers specialize in this type of food and it is just necessary for you to select the one best suited to your dog's needs. Active dogs have different requirements than more sedate dogs.

A Staffordshire Bull Terrier reaches adulthood between 18 and 24 months of age, though dogs will reach their full height by one year of age and continue "fill out" for the next 6 to 12 months.

Adult Staffords have different dietary needs than puppies. Additionaly, pregnant or nursing females will require a different diet than males.

DIETS FOR SENIOR DOGS

As dogs get older, their metabolism changes. The older dog usually exercises less, moves more slowly and sleeps more. This change in lifestyle and physiological performance requires a change in diet. Since these changes take place slowly, they might not be recognizable. What is easily recognizable is weight gain. By continuing to feed your dog an adult-maintenance diet when he is slowing down metabolically, your dog will gain weight. Obesity in an older dog compounds the health problems that already accompany old age.

As your dog gets older, few of his organs function up to par. The kidneys slow down and the intestines become less efficient. These age-related factors are best handled with a change in diet and a change in feeding schedule to give smaller portions that are more easily digested.

There is no single best diet for every older dog. While many dogs do well on light or senior diets, other dogs do better on special premium diets such as lamb and rice. Be sensitive to your senior Stafford's diet and this will help control other problems that may arise with your old friend.

TEST FOR PROPER DIET
A good test for proper diet is the color, odor and firmness of your dog's stool. A healthy dog usually produces three semi-hard stools per day. The stools should have no unpleasant odor. They should be the same color from excretion to excretion.

Your Stafford must always have fresh water available in a separate water bowl. The water should be changed daily and the bowl cleaned at the same time.

WATER

Just as your dog needs proper nutrition from his food, water is an essential "nutrient" as well. Water keeps the dog's body properly hydrated and promotes normal function of the body's systems. During housebreaking, it is necessary to keep an eye on how much water your Stafford is drinking and when, but, once he is reliably trained, he should have access to clean fresh water at all times. Make sure that the dog's water bowl is clean, and change the water often.

EXERCISE

All dogs require some form of exercise, regardless of breed. A sedentary lifestyle is as harmful to a dog as it is to a person. The Staffordshire Bull Terrier happens to have an above-average activity level and requires more exercise

The Stafford requires and enjoys exercise and activities. You'll enjoy it, too, as you'll continue to be amazed by this agile, athletic canine.

FEEDING TIPS

- Dog food must be served at room temperature, neither too hot nor too cold. Fresh water, changed often and served in a clean bowl, is mandatory, especially when feeding dry food.
- Never feed your dog from the table while you are eating, and never feed your dog leftovers from your own meal. They usually contain too much fat and too much seasoning.
- Dogs must chew their food. Hard pellets are excellent; soups and stews are to be avoided.
- Don't add leftovers or any extras to commercial dog food. The normal food is usually balanced, and adding something extra destroys the balance.
- Except for age-related changes, dogs do not require dietary variations. They can be fed the same diet, day after day, without their becoming bored or ill.

A Worthy Investment

Veterinary studies have proven that a balanced high-quality diet pays off in your dog's coat quality, behavior and activity level. Invest in premium brands for the maximum payoff with your dog.

THAT'S ENTERTAINMENT!

Is your dog home alone for much of the day? If you haven't taught him how to crochet or play the French horn, then he'll probably need something to occupy his paws and jaws, lest he turn to chewing the carpet. Recommended conditioning devices are toys that stimulate your dog both physically and mentally. Some of the most popular toys are those that are constructed to hide food inside. They provide not only a challenge but also instant gratification when your dog gets to the treat. Be sure to clean these carefully to prevent bacteria from building up.

than most breeds. Regular walks, play sessions in the yard or letting the dog run free in a secure area under your supervision are all sufficient forms of exercise for the Stafford. For those who are more ambitious, you will find that your Stafford will be able to keep up with you on extra-long walks or the morning run.

Keep in mind that not only is exercise essential to keep the dog's body fit, it is essential to his mental well-being. A bored dog will find something to do, which often manifests itself in some type of destructive behavior. In this sense, it is essential for the owner's mental well-being as well!

GROOMING

BRUSHING

A natural bristle brush or a hound glove can be used for regular routine brushing. Daily brushing is effective for removing dead hair and stimulating the dog's natural oils to add shine and a healthy look to the coat. Although the Stafford's coat is short and close, it does require a five-minute once-over to keep it looking its shiny best. Regular grooming sessions are also a good way to spend time with your dog. Many dogs grow to like the feel of being brushed and will enjoy the daily routine.

BATHING

Dogs do not need to be bathed as often as humans, but bathing as needed is important for healthy skin and a clean, shiny coat. Again, like most anything, if you accustom your pup to being bathed as a puppy, it will be second nature by the time he grows up. You want your dog to be at ease in the bath or else it could end up a wet, soapy, messy ordeal for both of you!

Make sure that your dog has a good non-slip surface to stand on. Begin by wetting the dog's coat. A shower or hose attachment is necessary for thoroughly wetting and rinsing the coat. Check the water temperature to make sure that it is neither too hot nor too cold for the dog.

Your local pet shop can offer a wide range of grooming tools. Fortunately, the Stafford requires little grooming besides the regular brushing, ear cleaning and nail clipping, and an occasional bath.

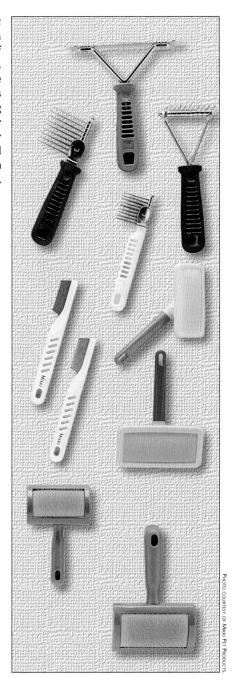

Photo courtesy of Mikki Pet Products.

Next, apply shampoo to the dog's coat and work it into a good lather. You should purchase a shampoo that is made for dogs. Do not use a product made for human hair. Wash the head last; you do not want shampoo to drip into the dog's eyes while you are washing the rest of his body. Work the shampoo all the way down to the skin. You can use this opportunity to check the skin for any bumps, bites or other abnormalities. Do not neglect any area of the body—get all of the hard-to-reach places.

Once the dog has been thoroughly shampooed, he requires an equally thorough rinsing. Shampoo left in the coat can be irritating to the skin. Protect his eyes from the shampoo by shielding them with your hand and directing the flow of water in the opposite direction. You should also avoid getting water in the ear canal. Be prepared for your dog to

SOAP IT UP
The use of human soap products like shampoo, bubble bath and hand soap can be damaging to a dog's coat and skin. Human products are too strong; they remove the protective oils coating the dog's hair and skin that make him water-resistant. Use only shampoo made especially for dogs. You may like to use a medicated shampoo, which will help to keep external parasites at bay.

shake out his coat—you might want to stand back, but make sure you have a hold on the dog to keep him from running through the house, and have a heavy towel ready.

EAR CLEANING

The ears should be kept clean and any excess hair inside the ear should be trimmed. Ears can be cleaned with a cotton ball and special liquid cleaner or ear powder made especially for dogs. Be on the lookout for any signs of infection or ear mite infestation. If your Stafford has been shaking his head or scratching at his ears frequently, this usually indicates a problem. If his ears have an unusual odor, this is a sure sign of mite infestation or infection, and a signal to have his ears checked by the veterinarian.

NAIL CLIPPING

Your Stafford should be accustomed to having his nails trimmed at an early age, since it will be part of your maintenance routine throughout his life. Not only does it look nicer, but a dog with long nails can cause injury if he scratches someone unintentionally. Also, a long nail has a better chance of ripping and bleeding, or of causing the feet to spread. A good rule of thumb is if you can hear your dog's nails' clicking on the floor when he walks, his nails are too long.

BATHING BEAUTY

Once you are sure that the dog is thoroughly rinsed, squeeze the excess water out of his coat with your hand and dry him with a heavy towel. You can then let the coat finish drying naturally. In cold weather, never allow your dog outside with a wet coat.

There are "dry bath" products on the market, which are sprays and powders intended for spot cleaning, that can be used between regular baths if necessary. They are not substitutes for regular baths, but they are easy to use for touch-ups as they do not require rinsing.

Your Stafford puppy's ears should be cleaned regularly, perhaps once a week. While cleaning, you should be gentle and alert for any signs of irritation or infection.

Before you start cutting, make sure you can identify the "quick" in each nail. The quick is a blood vessel that runs through the center of each nail and grows rather close to the end. It will bleed if accidentally cut, which will be quite painful for the dog as it contains nerve endings. Keep

Nail clipping is best accomplished with a special clipper made for use with dogs. Accustom the young pup to having his feet touched and nails clipped so that the dog doesn't object when he is older.

some type of clotting agent on hand, such as a styptic pencil or styptic powder (the type used for shaving). This will stop the bleeding quickly when applied to the end of the cut nail. Do not panic if this happens, just stop the bleeding and talk soothingly to your dog. Once he has calmed down, move on to the next nail. It is better to clip a little at a time, particularly with dark-nailed dogs.

Hold your pup steady as you begin trimming his nails; you do not want him to make any sudden movements or run away. Talk to him soothingly and stroke his fur as you clip. Holding him in your hand, simply take off the end of each nail in one quick clip. You should purchase nail clippers that are specially made for dogs; you can probably find them wherever you buy pet supplies.

Nail Clipping

Quick

Cut Line

Nail Casing

Walking on hard surfaces naturally wears down a dog's nails; thus, the dog will need to have his nails clipped less frequently.

DARK-COLORED NAIL

With black or dark nails, it's best to clip only a small bit of the nail at a time or to use a file where the quick is not visible.

LIGHT-COLORED NAIL

In light-colored nails, clipping is much simpler because you can see the vein (or quick) that grows inside the nail casing.

SAFE TRAVEL

When you travel with your dog, it's a good idea to take along water from home or to buy bottled water for the trip. In areas where water is sometimes chemically treated and sometimes comes right out of the ground, you can prevent adverse reactions to this essential part of your dog's diet.

The most extensive travel you do with your dog may be limited to trips to the vet's office—or you may decide to bring him along when the family goes on vacation. Whichever the case, it is important to consider your dog's safety and comfort while traveling.

"Let's hit the road!" says this happy traveler, although the back of a pickup truck is an extremely unsafe place for a dog to ride.

TRAVELING WITH YOUR DOG

CAR TRAVEL

You should accustom your Stafford to riding in the car at an early age. You may or may not take him in the car often, but at the very least he will need to go to the vet and you do not want these trips to be traumatic for the dog or a big hassle for you. The safest way for a dog to ride in the car is in his crate. If he uses a crate in the house, you can use the same crate for travel.

Put the pup in the crate and see how he reacts. If he seems uneasy, you can have a passenger hold him on his lap while you drive. Another option is a specially made safety harness for

dogs, which straps the dog in much like a seat belt. Do not let the dog roam loose in the vehicle—this is very dangerous! If you should stop short, your dog can be thrown and injured. If the dog starts climbing on you and pestering you while you are driving, you will not be able to concentrate on the road. It is an unsafe situation for everyone—human and canine.

For long trips, be prepared to stop to let the dog relieve himself. Bring along whatever you need to clean up after him. You should bring along some paper towels and old rags should he have an

accident in the car or become suffer from motion sickness.

A word or caution—*never* leave your dog alone in the car, not even for a minute! A car can heat up very quickly, even on cool days, and your dog could die from being closed in the vehicle. Leaving the window open is not a good idea either, as the dog can hurt himself trying to get out.

AIR TRAVEL

Contact your chosen airline before proceeding with travel plans that include your Stafford. The dog will be required to travel in a fiberglass crate and you should always check in advance with the airline regarding specific requirements for the crate's size, type and labeling, as well as any travel restrictions (such as during the summer months) and health certificates needed for the dog.

To help put your Stafford at ease for the trip, be sure he is well acclimated to the crate in which he will be traveling and give him

TRAVEL CAUTION

When traveling, never let your dog off-leash in a strange area. Your dog could run away out of fear, decide to chase a passing squirrel or cat or simply want to stretch his legs without restriction—if any of these happen, you might never see your canine friend again.

one of his favorite toys in the crate. Do not feed the dog for several hours prior to checking in so that you minimize his need to relieve himself. Some airlines require you to provide documentation as to when the dog was last fed. In any case, a light meal is best. For long trips, you will have to attach food and water bowls to the outside of the dog's crate so that airline employees can tend to him between legs of the trip.

Make sure that your dog is properly identified and that your contact information appears on his ID tags and on his crate. Your Stafford will travel in a different area of the plane than the human passengers, so every rule must be strictly followed to prevent any risk of getting separated from your dog.

VACATIONS AND BOARDING

So you want to take a family vacation—and you want to include *all* members of the family. You would probably make arrangements for accommodations ahead of time anyway, but this is especially important when traveling with a dog. You do not want to make an overnight stop at the only place around for miles and find out that the hotel does not allow dogs. Also, you do not want to reserve a place for your family without mentioning that you are bringing a dog because, if it is against the hotel's policy, you and

If your Stafford is accustomed to spending all his time with you and getting plenty of activity, the dog may not adjust very well to a boarding kennel when you decide to take a vacation.

your dog may end up without a place to stay.

Alternatively, if you are traveling and choose not to bring your Stafford, you will have to make arrangements for him while you are away. Some options are to bring him to a friend's house to stay while you are gone, to have a trusted neighbor stop by often or stay at your house or to bring your dog to a reputable boarding kennel. If you choose to board him at a kennel, you should stop by to see the facility and where the dogs are kept to make sure that it is clean. Talk to some of the employees and see how they treat the dogs—do they spend time with the dogs, play with

them, exercise them, etc.? You know that your Stafford will not be happy unless he gets regular activity. Also consider how your Stafford will react around strange dogs. Find out the kennel's policy on vaccinations and what they require. This is for all of the dogs' safety, since when dogs are kept together, there is a greater risk of diseases being passed from dog to dog.

LOST AND FOUND
You have a valuable dog. If the dog is lost or stolen, you would undoubtedly become extremely upset. Likewise, if you encounter a lost dog, notify the police or the local animal shelter.

IDENTIFICATION OPTIONS

As puppies become more and more expensive, especially those puppies of high quality for showing and/or breeding, they have a greater chance of being stolen. The usual collar dog tag is, of course, easily removed. But there are two more permanent techniques that have become widely used for identification.

The puppy microchip implantation involves the injection of a small microchip, about the size of a corn kernel, under the skin of the dog. If your dog shows up at a clinic or shelter, or is offered for resale under less-than-savory circumstances, he can be positively identified by the microchip. The microchip is scanned, and a registry quickly identifies you as the owner.

Tattooing is done on various parts of the dog, from his belly to his ears. The number tattooed can be your telephone number, your dog's registration number or any other number that you can easily memorize. When professional dog thieves see a tattooed dog, they usually lose interest. For the safety of our dogs, no laboratory facility or dog broker will accept a tattooed dog as stock.

Discuss microchipping and tattooing with your veterinarian and breeder. Some vets perform these services on their own premises for a reasonable fee. To ensure that your dog's identification is effective, be certain that he is then properly registered with a legitimate national database.

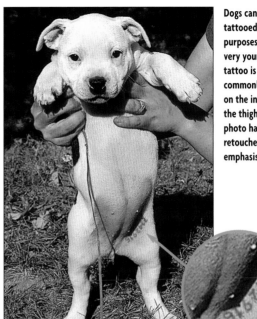

Dogs can be tattooed for ID purposes when very young. The tattoo is commonly done on the inside of the thigh. This photo has been retouched for emphasis.

IDENTIFICATION

Your Stafford is your valued companion and friend. That is why you always keep a close eye on him and you have made sure that he cannot escape from the yard or wriggle out of his collar and run away from you. However, accidents can happen and there may come a time when your dog unexpectedly gets separated from you. If this unfortunate event should occur, the first thing on your mind will be finding him. Proper identification, including an ID tag and possibly a tattoo and/or microchip, will increase the chances of his being returned to you safely and quickly.

STAFFORDSHIRE BULL TERRIER

Living with an untrained dog is a lot like owning a piano that you do not know how to play—it is a nice object to look at, but it does not do much more than that to bring you pleasure. Now try taking piano lessons, and suddenly the piano comes alive and brings forth magical sounds and rhythms that set your heart singing and your body swaying.

The same is true with your Staffordshire Bull Terrier. At first you enjoy seeing him around the house. He does not do much with you other than to need food, water and exercise. Come to think of it, he does not bring you much joy, either. He is a big responsibility with a very small return. Often he develops unacceptable behaviors that annoy and/or frustrate you, to say nothing of bad habits that may end up costing you great sums of money. Not a good thing!

Now train your Stafford. Enroll in an obedience class. Teach him good manners as you learn how and why he behaves the way he does. Find out how to communicate with your dog and how to recognize and understand his communications with you.

Suddenly the dog takes on a new role in your life—he is smart, interesting, well behaved and fun to be with. He demonstrates his bond of devotion to you daily. In other words, your Stafford does wonders for your ego because he constantly reminds you that you are not only his leader, you are his hero! Miraculous things have happened—you have a wonderful dog (even your family and friends have noticed the transformation!) and you feel good about yourself.

Those involved with teaching

(Opposite page) As cute and innocent as this Staffordshire pup looks, he can certainly cause a lot of trouble if not properly trained!

Staffordshire Bull Terriers are extremely intelligent dogs. They are readily trained and can bring much pleasure and happiness into the lives of their owners.

dog obedience and counseling owners about their dogs' behavior have discovered some interesting facts about dog ownership. For example, training dogs when they are puppies results in the highest rate of success in developing well-mannered and well-adjusted adult dogs. Training an older dog, from six months to six years of age, can produce almost equal results, providing that the owner accepts the dog's slower rate of learning capability and is willing to work patiently to help the dog succeed at developing to his fullest potential. Unfortunately, many owners of untrained adult dogs lack the patience factor, so they do not persist until their dogs are successful at learning particular behaviors.

Training a puppy aged 8 to 16 weeks (20 weeks at the most) is like working with a dry sponge in a pool of water. The pup soaks up whatever you show him and constantly looks for more things to do and learn. At this early age, his body is not yet producing hormones, and therein lies the reason for such a high rate of success. Without hormones, he is focused on his owners and not particularly interested in investigating other places, dogs, people, etc. You are his leader: his provider of food, water, shelter and security. He latches onto you and wants to stay close. He will usually follow you from room to

REAP THE REWARDS
If you start with a normal, healthy dog and give him time, patience and some carefully executed lessons, you will reap the rewards of that training for the life of the dog. And what a life it will be! The two of you will find immeasurable pleasure in the companionship you have built together with love, respect and understanding.

room, will not let you out of his sight when you are outdoors with him, and respond in like manner to the people and animals you encounter. If you greet a friend warmly, he will be happy to greet the person as well. If, however, you are hesitant or anxious about the approach of a stranger or other animal, he will respond accordingly.

Once the puppy begins to produce hormones, his natural curiosity emerges and he begins to investigate the world around him. It is at this time when you may notice that the untrained dog begins to wander away from you and even ignore your commands to stay close. When this behavior becomes a problem, the owner has two choices: get rid of the dog or train him. It is strongly urged that you choose the latter option.

Occasionally there will not be obedience classes available within a reasonable distance from your home. Sometimes there are classes available, but the tuition is too costly. Whatever the circumstances, the solution to training your Staffordshire Bull Terrier without formal obedience classes lies within the pages of this book.

This chapter is devoted to helping you train your Stafford at home. If the recommended procedures are followed faithfully, you may expect positive results that will prove rewarding to both you and your dog.

Whether your Stafford is a puppy or a mature adult, the methods of teaching and the techniques we use in training basic behaviors are the same. After all,

During training, such as this sit exercise, you must maintain your Stafford's attention. If the dog is constantly distracted, you will have a problem training and controlling the dog.

no dog, whether puppy or adult, likes harsh or inhumane methods. All creatures, however, respond favorably to gentle motivational methods and sincere praise and encouragement. Now let us get started.

HOUSEBREAKING

You can train a puppy to relieve himself wherever you choose. For example, city dwellers often train their puppies to relieve themselves along the curbside because large plots of grass are not readily available. Suburbanites, on the other hand, usually have yards to accommodate their dogs' needs.

Outdoor training includes such surfaces as grass, dirt and cement. Indoor training usually means training your dog to newspaper (not a very good option for Stafford owners). When deciding on the surface and location that

---

LANGUAGE BARRIER

Dogs do not understand our language and have to rely on tone of voice more than just words or sound. They can be trained to react to a certain sound, at a certain volume. If you say "No, Oliver" in a very soft, pleasant voice, it will not have the same meaning as "No, Oliver!!" when you raise your voice.

You should never use the dog's name during a reprimand, just the command "No! " You never want the dog to associate his name with a negative experience or reprimand.

Your Stafford's relief site depends upon the area that your choose for him. You'd be wise to choose an out-of-the way grassy spot rather than your patio.

you will want your Stafford to use, be sure it is going to be permanent. Training your dog to grass and then changing your mind a few months later is extremely difficult for both dog and owner.

Next, choose the command you will use each and every time you want your puppy to void. "Hurry up" and "Let's go" are examples of commands commonly used by dog owners. Get in the habit of asking the puppy, "Do you want to go hurry up?" (or whatever your chosen relief command is) before you take him out. That way, when he becomes an adult, you will be able to determine if he wants to go out when you ask him. A confirmation will be signs of interest such as wagging his tail, watching you intently, going to the door, etc.

PUPPY'S NEEDS

Your puppy needs to relieve himself after play periods, after each meal, after he has been sleeping and any time he indicates that he is looking for a place to urinate or defecate. The urinary and intestinal tract muscles of very young puppies are not fully developed. Therefore, like human babies, puppies need to relieve themselves frequently.

Take your puppy out often—every hour for an eight-week-old, for example. The older the puppy, the less often he will need to relieve himself. Finally, as a mature healthy adult, he will require only three to five relief trips per day.

HOUSING

Since the types of housing and control you provide for your puppy have a direct relationship

PLAN TO PLAY
The puppy should also have regular play and exercise sessions when he is with you or a family member. Exercise for a very young puppy can consist of a short walk around the house or yard. Playing can include fetching games with a large ball or a special toy. (All puppies teethe and need soft things upon which to chew.) Remember to restrict play periods to indoors within his living area (the family room, for example) until he is completely house-trained.

HOW MANY TIMES A DAY?

AGE	RELIEF TRIPS
To 14 weeks	10
14–22 weeks	8
22–32 weeks	6
Adulthood	4
(dog stops growing)	

These are estimates, of course, but they are a guide to the *minimum* number of opportunities a dog should have each day to relieve himself.

on the success of house-training, we consider the various aspects of both before we begin training.

Bringing a new puppy home and turning him loose in your house can be compared to turning a child loose in an amusement park and telling the child that the place is all his! The sheer enormity of the place would be too much for him to handle.

Instead, offer the puppy clearly defined areas where he can play, sleep, eat and live. A room of the house where the family gathers is the most obvious choice. Puppies are social animals and need to feel a part of the pack right from the start. Hearing your voice, watching you while you are doing things and smelling you nearby are all positive reinforcers that he is now a member of your pack. Usually a family room, the kitchen or a nearby adjoining breakfast nook is ideal for provid-

ing safety and security for both puppy and owner.

Within that room, there should be a smaller area that the puppy can call his own. A wire or fiberglass dog crate or a partitioned-off (not boarded!) corner from which he can view the activities of his new family will be fine. The size of the area or crate is the key factor here. The area must be large enough for the puppy to lie down and stretch out as well as stand up without rubbing his head on the top, yet small enough so that he cannot relieve himself at one end and sleep at the other without coming into contact with his droppings. Dogs are, by nature, clean animals and will not remain close to their relief areas unless forced to do so. In those cases, they then become dirty dogs and usually remain that way for life.

Before the pups are old enough to relieve themselves outdoors, the breeder must provide them with a suitable "toilet" area.

The crate or area should be lined with clean bedding and offer one toy, no more. Do not put food or water in the crate during the housebreaking process, as eating and drinking will activate his digestive processes and ultimately defeat your purpose as well as make the puppy very uncomfortable as he attempts to "hold it."

CONTROL

By control, we mean helping the puppy to create a lifestyle pattern that will be compatible to that of his human pack *(you!)*. Just as we guide little children to learn our way of life, we must show the puppy when it is time to play, eat, sleep, exercise and even entertain himself.

Your puppy should always sleep in his crate. He should also learn that, during times of household confusion and excessive

PAPER CAPER
Never line your pup's sleeping area with newspaper. Puppy litters are usually raised on newspaper and, once in your home, the puppy will immediately associate newspaper with voiding. Never put newspaper on any floor while house-training, as this will only confuse the puppy. Finally, restrict water intake after evening meals; offer a few licks at a time. Never let your Stafford gulp water after meals.

To a Stafford, his home is his castle. Staffords must have a place they can recognize as their own. This dog house provides a safe haven for these two Stafford chums while out in the yard.

human activity such as at breakfast when family members are preparing for the day, he can play by himself in relative safety and comfort in his crate. Each time you leave the puppy alone, he should be crated.

Puppies are chewers. They cannot tell the difference between things like lamp cords, television wires, shoes, table legs, etc. Chewing into a television wire,

TAKE THE LEAD

Do not carry your dog to his relief area. Lead him there on a leash or, better yet, encourage him to follow you to the spot. If you start carrying him to his spot, you might end up doing this routine forever and your dog will have the satisfaction of having trained *you*.

for example, can be fatal to the puppy, while a shorted wire can start a fire in the house. Crating the puppy when you're not around prevents potential dangers.

If the puppy chews on the arm of the chair when he is alone, you will probably discipline him angrily when you get home. Thus, he makes the association that your coming home means he is going to be punished. (He will not remember chewing up the chair and is incapable of making the association of the discipline with his naughty deed.) Crating the puppy when you can't supervise also prevents him from engaging in destructive behavior.

Times of excitement, such as family parties, etc., can be fun for the puppy, providing he can view the activities from the security of his crate. He is not underfoot and he is not being fed all sorts of tidbits that will probably cause him stomach distress, yet he still feels a part of the fun.

Don't let your puppy "lie down on the job." Teach him to do his business quickly when you take him out for relief.

SCHEDULE

As stated earlier, a puppy should be taken to his relief area each time he is released from his crate, after meals, after play sessions, when he first awakens in the morning (at age 8 weeks, this can mean 5 a.m.!) and whenever he indicates by circling or sniffing busily that he needs to urinate or defecate. For a puppy less than ten weeks of age, a routine of taking him out every hour is necessary. As the puppy grows, he will be able to wait for longer periods of time.

THE SUCCESS METHOD

Success that comes by luck is usually short-lived. Success that comes by well-thought-out proven methods is often more easily achieved and permanent. This is the Success Method. It is designed to give you, the puppy owner, a simple yet proven way to help your puppy develop clean living habits and a feeling of security in his new environment.

6 Steps to Successful Crate Training

1 Tell the puppy "Crate time!" and place him in the crate with a small treat (a piece of cheese or half of a biscuit). Let him stay in the crate for five minutes while you are in the same room. Then release him and praise lavishly. Never release him when he is fussing. Wait until he is quiet before you let him out.

2 Repeat Step 1 several times a day.

3 The next day, place the puppy in the crate as before. Let him stay there for ten minutes. Do this several times.

4 Continue building time in five-minute increments until the puppy stays in his crate for 30 minutes with you in the room. Always take him to his relief area after prolonged periods in his crate.

5 Now go back to Step 1 and let the puppy stay in his crate for five minutes, this time while you are out of the room.

6 Once again, build crate time in five-minute increments with you out of the room. When the puppy will stay willingly in his crate (he may even fall asleep!) for 30 minutes with you out of the room, he will be ready to stay in it for several hours at a time.

Keep trips to his relief area short. Stay no more than five or six minutes and then return to the house. If he goes during that time, praise him lavishly and take him indoors immediately. If he does not, but he has an accident when you go back indoors, pick him up immediately, say "No! No!" and return to his relief area. Wait a few minutes, then return to the house again. *Never* hit a puppy or put his face in urine or excrement when he has an accident!

Once indoors, put the puppy in his crate until you have had time to clean up his accident. Then release him to the family area and watch him more closely than before. Chances are, his accident was a result of your not picking up his signal or waiting too long before offering him the opportunity to relieve himself. *Never* hold a grudge against the puppy for accidents.

A durable fiberglass crate is ideal for your Stafford when traveling, though wire crates are preferred for everyday use in the home.

Let the puppy learn that going outdoors means it is time to relieve himself, not to play. Once trained, he will be able to play indoors and out and still differentiate between the times for play versus the times for relief.

Help the puppy develop regular hours for naps, being alone, playing by himself and just resting, all in his crate. Encourage him to entertain himself while you are busy with your activities. Let him learn that having you near is comforting, but it is not your main purpose in life to provide him with undivided attention.

Each time you put your puppy in his crate tell him, "Crate time!" (or whatever command you choose). Soon, he will run to his crate when he hears you say those words.

In the beginning of his training, do not leave him in his crate

THE CLEAN LIFE

By providing sleeping and resting quarters that fit the dog, and offering frequent opportunities to relieve himself outside his quarters, the puppy quickly learns that the outdoors is the place to go when he needs to urinate or defecate. It also reinforces his innate desire to keep his sleeping quarters clean. This, in turn, helps develop the muscle control that will eventually produce a dog with clean living habits.

House-training males is more difficult than females. Male Staffords mark their territory on trees, bushes, and any other vertical object —fire hydrants are a traditional favorite!

for prolonged periods of time except during the night when everyone is sleeping. Make his experience with his crate a pleasant one and, as an adult, he will love his crate and willingly stay

Your Stafford should have a crate large enough for him to stand comfortably. A sturdy crate will even support the weight of a young friend!

in it for several hours. There are millions of people who go to work every day and leave their adult dogs crated while they are away. The dogs accept this as their lifestyle and look forward to "crate time."

Crate training provides safety for you, the puppy and the home. It also provides the puppy with a feeling of security, and that helps the puppy achieve self-confidence and clean habits. Remember that one of the primary ingredients in house-training your puppy is control. Regardless of your lifestyle, there will always be occasions when you will need to have a place where your dog can stay and be happy and safe. Crate training is the answer for now and in the future.

In conclusion, a few key elements are really all you need for a successful house-training method—consistency, frequency, praise, control and supervision. By following these procedures with a normal, healthy puppy, you and the puppy will soon be past the stage of "accidents" and ready to move on to a clean and rewarding life together.

ROLES OF DISCIPLINE, REWARD AND PUNISHMENT
Discipline, training one to act in accordance with rules, brings order to life. It is as simple as that. Without discipline, particularly in a group society, chaos

CANINE DEVELOPMENT SCHEDULE

It is important to understand how and at what age a puppy develops into adulthood. If you are a puppy owner, consult the following Canine Development Schedule to determine the stage of development your puppy is currently experiencing. This knowledge will help you as you work with the puppy in the weeks and months ahead.

Period	Age	Characteristics
FIRST TO THIRD	BIRTH TO SEVEN WEEKS	Puppy needs food, sleep and warmth, and responds to simple and gentle touching. Needs mother for security and disciplining. Needs littermates for learning and interacting with other dogs. Pup learns to function within a pack and learns pack order of dominance. Begin socializing pup with adults and children for short periods. Pup begins to become aware of his environment.
FOURTH	EIGHT TO TWELVE WEEKS	Brain is fully developed. Pup needs socializing with outside world. Remove from mother and littermates. Needs to change from canine pack to human pack. Human dominance necessary. Fear period occurs between 8 and 12 weeks. Avoid fright and pain.
FIFTH	THIRTEEN TO SIXTEEN WEEKS	Training and formal obedience should begin. Less association with other dogs, more with people, places, situations. Period will pass easily if you remember this is pup's change-to-adolescence time. Be firm and fair. Flight instinct prominent. Permissiveness and over-disciplining can do permanent damage. Praise for good behavior.
JUVENILE	FOUR TO EIGHT MONTHS	Another fear period about 7 to 8 months of age. It passes quickly, but be cautious of fright and pain. Sexual maturity reached. Dominant traits established. Dog should understand sit, down, come and stay by now.

NOTE: THESE ARE APPROXIMATE TIME FRAMES. ALLOW FOR INDIVIDUAL DIFFERENCES IN PUPPIES.

reigns supreme and the group will eventually perish. Humans and canines are social animals and need some form of discipline in order to function effectively. They must procure food, reproduce to keep the species going and protect their home base and their young.

If there were no discipline in the lives of social animals, they would eventually die from starvation and/or predation by other stronger animals. In the case of domestic canines, dogs need discipline in their lives in order to understand how their pack (you and other family members) function and how they must act in order to survive.

A large humane society in a highly populated area recently surveyed dog owners regarding their satisfaction with their relationships with their dogs. People who had trained their dogs were 75% more satisfied with their pets than those who had never trained their dogs.

Dr. Edward Thorndike, a noted psychologist, established *Thorndike's Theory of Learning*, which states that a behavior that results in a pleasant event tends to be repeated. A behavior that results in an unpleasant event tends not to be repeated. It is this theory on which training methods are based today. For example, if you manipulate a dog to perform a specific behavior and reward him for doing it, he is likely to do it

TRAINING RULES
If you want to be successful in training your dog, you have four rules to obey yourself:
1. Develop an understanding of how a dog thinks.
2. Do not blame the dog for lack of communication.
3. Define your dog's personality and act accordingly.
4. Have patience and be consistent.

again because he enjoyed the end result.

Occasionally, punishment, a penalty inflicted for an offense, is necessary. The best type of punishment often comes from an outside source. For example, a child is told not to touch the stove because he may get burned. He disobeys and touches the stove. In doing so, he receives a burn. From that time on, he respects the heat of the stove and avoids contact with it. Therefore, a behavior that results in an unpleasant event tends not to be repeated.

A good example of a dog's learning the hard way is the dog who chases the house cat. He is told many times to leave the cat alone, yet he persists in teasing the family cat. Then, one day he begins chasing the cat but the cat turns and swipes a claw across the dog's face, leaving him with a painful gash on his nose. The final result is that the dog stops chasing the cat.

TRAINING EQUIPMENT

COLLAR
A simple buckle collar is fine for most dogs. One who pulls mightily on the leash may require a chain choker collar, only if the owner has been instructed in the proper use of this type of collar. Some owners prefer to use harnesses when walking their Staffords.

LEASH
About a 6-foot leash is recommended, preferably made of leather, nylon or heavy cloth. A chain leash is not recommended, as many dog owners find that the chain cuts into their hands and that frequently switching the leash back and forth between their hands is painful.

TREATS
Have a bag of treats on hand. Something nutritious and easy to swallow works best. Use a soft treat, a chunk of cheese or a piece of cooked chicken rather than a dry biscuit. By the time the dog gets done chewing a dry treat, he will forget why he is being rewarded in the first place!

Using food rewards will not teach a dog to beg at the table—the only way to teach a dog to beg at the table is to give him food from the table. In training, rewarding the dog with a food treat will help him associate

THE GOLDEN RULE
The golden rule of dog training is simple. For each "question" (command), there is only one correct answer (reaction). One command = one reaction. Keep practicing the command until the dog reacts correctly without hesitating. Be repetitive but not monotonous. Dogs get bored just as people do!

praise and the treats with learning new behaviors that obviously please his owner.

TRAINING BEGINS: ASK THE DOG A QUESTION
In order to teach your dog anything, you must first get his attention. After all, he cannot learn anything if he is looking away from you with his mind on something else.

To get his attention, ask him "School?" and immediately walk

Choose a collar that fits your Stafford comfortably, neither too tight and restrictive nor too loose, for danger of his slipping out of it.

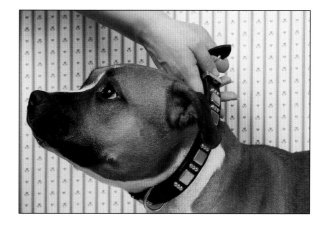

CHOOSE AN APPROPRIATE COLLAR

The **BUCKLE COLLAR** is the standard collar used for everyday purposes. Be sure that you adjust the buckle on growing puppies. Check it every day. It can become too tight overnight! These collars can be made of leather or nylon. Attach your dog's identification tags to this collar.

The **CHOKE COLLAR** is designed for training. It is constructed of highly polished steel so that it slides easily through the stainless steel loop. The idea is that the dog controls the pressure around his neck and he will stop pulling if the collar becomes uncomfortable. It must be used properly and *never* left on your dog when not training.

The **HALTER** is for a trained dog that has to be restrained to prevent running away, chasing a cat and the like. Considered the most humane of all collars, it is frequently used on smaller dogs on which collars are not comfortable.

over to him and give him a treat as you tell him "Good dog." Wait a minute or two and repeat the routine, this time with a treat in your hand as you approach within a foot of the dog. Do not go directly to him, but stop about a foot short of him and hold out the treat as you ask "School?" He will see you approaching with a treat in your hand and most likely begin walking toward you. As you meet, give him the treat and praise again.

The third time, ask the question, have a treat in your hand and walk only a short distance toward the dog so that he must walk almost all the way to you. As he reaches you, give him the treat and praise again.

By this time, the dog will probably be getting the idea that if he pays attention to you, especially when you ask that question, it will pay off in treats and fun activities for him. In other words, he learns that "school" means doing fun things with you that result in treats and positive attention for him.

Remember that the dog does not understand your verbal

Never underestimate the power of food! Make your Stafford sit and stay before presenting him with his meal. This structure and discipline sets the tone of your leadership role.

language, he only recognizes sounds. Your question translates to a series of sounds for him, and those sounds become the signal to go to you and pay attention; if he does, he will get to interact with you plus receive treats and praise.

THE BASIC COMMANDS

TEACHING SIT

Now that you have the dog's attention, attach his leash and hold it in your left hand and a food treat in your right. Place your food hand at the dog's nose and let him lick the treat but not take it from you. Say "Sit" and slowly raise your food hand from in front of the dog's nose up over his head so that he is looking at the ceiling.

OPEN MINDS

Dogs are as different from each other as people are. What works for one dog may not work for another. Have an open mind. If one method of training is unsuccessful, try another.

As he bends his head upward, he will have to bend his knees to maintain his balance. As he bends his knees, he will assume a sit position. At that point, release the food treat and praise lavishly with comments such as "Good dog! Good sit!," etc. Remember to always praise enthusiastically, because dogs relish verbal praise from their owners and feel so proud of themselves whenever they accomplish a behavior.

Incidentally, you will not use food forever in getting the dog to obey your commands. Food is only used to teach new behaviors, and once the dog knows what you want when you give a specific command, you will wean him off of the food treats but still maintain the verbal praise. After all, you will always have your voice with you, and there will be many times when you have no food rewards but expect the dog to obey.

Teaching Down

Teaching the down exercise is easy when you understand how the dog perceives the down position, and it is very difficult when you do not. Dogs perceive the down position as a submissive one. Therefore, teaching the down exercise using a forceful method can sometimes make the dog develop such a fear of the down that he either runs away when you say "down" or he attempts to

COMMAND STANCE
Stand up straight and authoritatively when giving your dog commands. Do not issue commands when lying on the floor or lying on your back on the sofa. If you are on your hands and knees when you give a command, your dog will think you are positioning yourself to play.

bite the person who tries to force him down.

Have the dog sit close along-side your left leg, facing in the same direction as you are. Hold the leash in your left hand and a food treat in your right. Now place your left hand lightly on the top of the dog's shoulders where they meet above the spinal cord. Do not push down on the dog's shoulders; simply rest your left hand there so you can guide the dog to lie down close to your left leg rather than to swing away from your side when he drops.

Now place the food hand at the dog's nose, say "Down" very softly (almost a whisper) and slowly lower the food hand to the dog's front feet. When the food hand reaches the floor, begin moving it forward along the floor in front of the dog. Keep talking softly to the dog, saying things

A Stafford is a girl's best friend! We promised little Jaime to mention her name if she posed with her Stafford Little Bug.

like, "Do you want this treat? You can do this, good dog." Your reassuring tone of voice will help calm the dog as he tries to follow the food hand in order to get the treat.

When the dog's elbows touch the floor, release the food and praise softly. Try to get the dog to maintain that down position for

PARENTAL GUIDANCE

Training a dog is a life experience. Many parents admit that much of what they know about raising children they learned from caring for their dogs. Dogs respond to love, fairness and guidance, just as children do. Become a good dog owner and you may become an even better parent.

several seconds before you let him sit up again. The goal here is to get the dog to settle down and not feel threatened in the down position.

TEACHING STAY

It is easy to teach the dog to stay in either a sit or a down position. Again, we use food and praise during the teaching process as we help the dog to understand exactly what it is that we are expecting him to do.

To teach the sit/stay, start with the dog sitting on your left side as before and hold the leash in your left hand. Have a food treat in your right hand and place your food hand at the dog's nose. Say "Stay" and step out on your

Treats are excellent motivation during training exercises. Pet shops sell a variety of dog treats, or small pieces of cheese or other healthy tidbits will suffice.

right foot to stand directly in front of the dog, toe to toe, as he licks and nibbles the treat. Be sure to keep his head facing upward to maintain the sit position. Count to five and then swing around to stand next to the dog again with him on your left. As soon as you get back to the original position, release the food and praise lavishly.

To teach the down/stay, do the down as previously described. As soon as the dog lies down, say "Stay" and step out on your right foot just as you did in the sit/stay. Count to five and then return to stand beside the dog with him on your left side. Release the treat and praise as always.

Within a week or ten days, you can begin to add a bit of distance between you and your dog when you leave him. When you do, use your left hand open with the palm facing the dog as a stay signal, much the same as the hand signal a police officer uses to stop traffic at an intersection. Hold the food treat in your right

hand as before, but this time the food is not touching the dog's nose. He will watch the food hand and quickly learn that he is going to get that treat as soon as you return to his side.

When you can stand 3 feet away from your dog for 30 seconds, you can then begin building time and distance in both stays. Eventually, the dog can be expected to remain in the stay position for prolonged periods of time until you return to him or call him to you. Always praise lavishly when he stays.

TEACHING COME

If you make teaching the come exercise a fun experience, you should never have a student that does not love the game or that fails to come when called. The secret, it seems, is never to teach the word "come."

At times when an owner most wants his dog to come when

CALM DOWN

Dogs will do anything for your attention. If you reward the dog when he is calm and attentive, you will develop a well-mannered dog. If, on the other hand, you greet your dog excitedly and encourage him to wrestle and roughhouse with you, the dog will greet you the same way and you will have a hyper dog on your hands.

Entice your Stafford with a taste, but don't let him take the treat until he has completed the exercise.

dog's success at locating him. Once the dog learns to love the game, simply calling out "Where are you?" will bring him running from wherever he is when he hears that all-important question.

The come command is recognized as one of the most important things to teach a dog, but there are trainers who work with thousands of dogs and never teach the actual word "Come." Yet these dogs will race to respond to a person who uses the dog's name followed by "Where are you?" For example, a woman has a 12-year-old companion dog who went blind, but who never fails to locate her owner when asked, "Where are you?"

called, the owner is likely upset or anxious and he allows these feelings to come through in the tone of his voice when he calls his dog. Hearing that desperation in his owner's voice, the dog fears the results of going to him and therefore either disobeys outright or runs in the opposite direction. The secret, therefore, is to teach the dog a game and, when you want him to come to you, simply play the game. It is practically a no-fail solution!

To begin, have several members of your family take a few food treats and each go into a different room in the house. Take turns calling the dog, and each person should celebrate the dog's finding him with a treat and lots of happy praise. When a person calls the dog, he is actually inviting the dog to find him and get a treat as a reward for "winning."

A few turns of the "Where are you?" game and the dog will figure out that everyone is playing the game and that each person has a big celebration awaiting the

PRACTICE MAKES PERFECT!

- Have training lessons with your dog every day in several short segments—three to five times a day for a few minutes at a time is ideal.
- Do not have long practice sessions. The dog will become easily bored.
- Never practice when you are tired, ill, worried or in an otherwise negative mood. This will transmit to the dog and may have an adverse effect on his performance.

  Think fun, short and above all *positive!* End each session on a high note, rather than a failed exercise, and make sure to give a lot of praise. Enjoy the training and help your dog enjoy it, too.

Children particularly love to play this game with their dogs. Children can hide in smaller places like a shower or bathtub, behind a bed or under a table. The dog needs to work a little bit harder to find these hiding places, but when he does he loves to celebrate with a treat and a tussle with a favorite youngster.

TEACHING HEEL

Heeling means that the dog walks beside the owner without pulling. It takes time and patience on the owner's part to succeed at teaching the dog that he (the owner) will not proceed unless the dog is walking calmly beside him. Pulling out ahead on the leash is definitely not acceptable.

Begin with holding the leash in your left hand as the dog sits beside your left leg. Move the loop end of the leash to your right hand but keep your left hand short on the leash so it keeps the dog in close to you.

Say "Heel" and step forward on your left foot. Keep the dog close to you and take three steps. Stop and have the dog sit next to you in what we now call the heel position. Praise verbally, but do not touch the dog. Hesitate a moment and begin again with "Heel," taking three steps and stopping, at which point the dog is told to sit again.

Your goal here is to have the dog walk those three steps with-

> ### "COME" . . . BACK
> Never call your dog to come to you for a correction or scold him when he reaches you. That is the quickest way to turn a come command into "Go away fast!" Dogs think only in the present tense, and your dog will connect the scolding with coming to you, not with the misbehavior of a few moments earlier.

out pulling on the leash. When he will walk calmly beside you for three steps without pulling, increase the number of steps you take to five. When he will walk politely beside you while you take five steps, you can increase the length of your walk to ten steps. Keep increasing the length of your stroll until the dog will walk quietly beside you without pulling as long as you want him to heel. When you stop heeling, indicate to the dog that the exercise is over by verbally praising as you pet him and say "OK, good dog." The "OK" is used as a release word, meaning that the exercise is finished and the dog is free to relax.

If you are dealing with a dog who insists on pulling you around, simply "put on your brakes" and stand your ground until the dog realizes that the two of you are not going anywhere until he is beside you and moving at your pace, not his. It may take some time just standing there to

Staffords are very active and can enjoy all kinds of things with their owners, from chores around the house to hiking in the hills.

convince the dog that you are the leader and you will be the one to decide on the direction and speed of your travel.

Each time the dog looks up at you or slows down to give a slack leash between the two of you, quietly praise him and say, "Good heel. Good dog." Eventually, the dog will begin to respond and within a few days he will be walking politely beside you without pulling on the leash. At first, the training sessions should be

---

TUG OF WALK?

If you begin teaching the heel by taking long walks and letting the dog pull you along, he misinterprets this action as an acceptable form of taking a walk. When you pull back on the leash to counteract his pulling, he reads that tug as a signal to pull even harder!

HEELING WELL

Teach your dog to heel in an enclosed area. Once you think the dog will obey reliably and you want to attempt advanced obedience exercises such as off-lead heeling, test him in a fenced-in area so he cannot run away.

Training a dog to accept treats for the successful execution of commands is simple. Weaning them off food bribes is more difficult.

kept short and very positive; soon the dog will be able to walk nicely with you for increasingly longer distances. Remember also to give the dog free time and the opportunity to run and play when you are done with heel practice.

WEANING OFF FOOD IN TRAINING

Food is used in training new behaviors. Once the dog understands what behavior goes with a specific command, it is time to start weaning him off the food treats. At first, give a treat after each exercise. Then, start to give a treat only after every other exercise. Mix up the times when you offer a food reward and the times when you only offer praise so that the dog will never know when he is going to receive both food and praise and when he is going to receive only praise. This is called a variable-ratio reward system and it proves successful because there is always the chance that the owner will produce a treat, so the dog never stops trying for that reward. No matter what, *always* give verbal praise.

OBEDIENCE CLASSES

As previously discussed, it is a good idea to enroll in an obedience class if one is available in your area. If yours is a show dog, handling classes would be appropriate. Many areas have dog clubs that offer basic obedience training as well as preparatory classes for obedience competition. There are also local dog trainers who offer similar classes.

At obedience trials, dogs can earn titles at various levels of competition. The beginning levels of competition include basic behaviors such as sit, down, heel, etc. The more advanced levels of competition include jumping, retrieving, scent discrimination and signal work. The advanced levels require a dog and owner to put a lot of time and effort into their training, and the titles that can be earned at these levels of competition are very prestigious.

OTHER ACTIVITIES FOR LIFE
Whether a dog is trained in the structured environment of a class or alone with his owner at home, there are many activities that can

> **FETCH!**
> Play fetching games with your puppy in an enclosed area where he can retrieve his toy and bring it back to you. Always use a toy or object designated just for this purpose. Never use a shoe, sock or other item he may later confuse with those in your closet or underneath your chair.

bring fun and rewards to both owner and dog once they have mastered basic control.

Teaching the dog to help out around the home, in the yard or on the farm provides great satis-

Enrolling your Stafford in an obedience class may be the best choice you can make in training your dog. When properly instructed, Staffords can shine in every area of obedience, and the experience of being socialized with other dogs is good for them.

Can you believe that a Staffordshire Bull Terrier in good physical condition can jump as high as a man? Staffords enjoy the challenge of intense physical training.

HELPING PAWS

Your dog may not be the next Lassie, but every pet has the potential to do some tricks well. Identify his natural talents and hone them. Is your dog always happy and upbeat? Teach him to wag his tail or give you his paw on command. Real homebodies can be trained to do household chores, such as carrying dirty laundry or retrieving the morning paper.

faction to both dog and owner. In addition, the dog's help makes life a little easier for his owner and raises his stature as a valued companion to his family. It helps give the dog a purpose by occupying his mind and providing an outlet for his energy.

Backpacking is an exciting and healthful activity that the dog can be taught without assistance from more than his owner. The exercise of walking and climbing is good for man and dog alike, and the bond that they develop together is priceless. The rule of thumb for backpacking is never to let the dog carry more than one-sixth of his body weight.

If you are interested in participating in organized competition with your Staffordshire Bull Terrier, there are activities other than obedience in which you and your dog can become involved. Agility is a popular and fun sport where dogs run through an obstacle course that includes various jumps, tunnels and other exercises to test the dog's speed and coordination. The owners often run through the course beside their dogs to give commands and to guide them through the course. Although competitive, the focus is on fun—it's fun to do, fun to watch, and great exercise.

As a Staffordshire Bull Terrier owner, you have the opportunity to participate in Schutzhund competition if you choose. Schutzhund originated as a test to determine the best-quality German Shepherd to be used for breeding stock. Now it is open to other breeds as well, and breeders continue to use it as a way to evaluate working ability and temperament. There are three levels in Schutzhund trials: SchH. I, SchH. II and SchH. III, with each level being progressively more difficult to complete successfully. Each level consists of training, obedience and protection phases. Training for Schutzhund is intense and must be practiced consistently to keep the dog keen. The experience of Schutzhund training is very rewarding for dog and owner, and the Stafford's tractability is well suited for this type of training.

MEDICAL PROBLEMS SEEN IN
STAFFORDSHIRE BULL TERRIERS

Condition	Age Affected	Cause	Area Affected
Acral Lick Granuloma	Any age	Unknown	Legs
Bilateral Cataracts	Younger dogs	Inherited	Eye
Cleft Palate/Harelip	Newborns	Congenital	Hard or soft palate
Elbow Dysplasia	4 to 7 mos.	Congenital	Elbow joint
Gastric Dilatation (Bloat)	Any age	Swallowing air	Stomach
Hip Dysplasia	4 to 9 mos.	Congenital	Hip joint
Patellar Luxation	Any age	Congenital or acquired	Kneecaps
Progressive Retinal Atrophy	Older dogs	Inherited	Retina
Urolithiasis	Adult	Cystine uroliths/stones	Kidney/Bladder
Von Willebrand's Disease	Birth	Congenital	Blood

STAFFORDSHIRE BULL TERRIER

Dogs suffer from many of the same physical illnesses as people. They might even share many of the same psychological problems. Since people usually know more about human diseases than canine maladies, many of the terms used in this chapter will be familiar, but not necessarily those used by veterinarians. We'll use the term *x-ray*, instead of the more acceptable term *radiograph*. We will also use the familiar term *symptoms* even though dogs don't have symptoms, which are are verbal descriptions of the patient's feelings. Since dogs can't speak, we have to look for *clinical signs*...but we still use the term *symptoms* in this book.

As a general rule, medicine is *practiced*. That term is not arbitrary. Medicine is a constantly changing art as we learn more and more about genetics, electronic aids (like CAT scans and MRI scans) and different opinions. There are many dog maladies, like hip dysplasia, which are not universally treated in the same manner. For example, some veterinarians opt for surgical treatment more often than others.

SELECTING A QUALIFIED VET

Your selection of a veterinarian should be based upon personality and skills with dogs as well as his convenience to your home. You want a vet who is close, as you might have emergencies or need to make multiple visits for treatments. You want a vet who has services that you might require such as a boarding kennel and tattooing, and of course a good reputation for ability and responsiveness. There is nothing more frustrating than having to wait to get a response from a veterinarian.

All veterinarians are licensed and should be capable of dealing with routine health issues. Most veterinarians do routine surgery such as neutering, stitching up

A veterinarian examining an x-ray. You should choose a vet before bringing your Stafford puppy home.

wounds and docking tails for those breeds in which such is required for show purposes. There are, however, many veterinary specialties that require further studies and internships. These include specialists in heart problems (veterinary cardiologists), skin problems (veterinary dermatologists), teeth and gum problems (veterinary dentists), eye problems (veterinary ophthalmologists) and x-rays (veterinary radiologists), and surgeons who have specialties in bones, muscles or certain organs.

When the problem affecting your dog is serious, your vet will refer you to someone in the relevant field. It is not unusual or impudent to get another medical opinion, although it is courteous to advise the vets concerned. You might also want to compare costs among several veterinarians. Sophisticated health care and veterinary services can be very costly. Don't be bashful about discussing these costs with your veterinarian. It is not infrequent that important decisions about treatment options are based upon financial considerations.

PREVENTATIVE MEDICINE
It is much easier, less costly and more effective to practice preventative medicine than to fight bouts of illness and disease. Properly bred puppies come from parents that were selected based upon their genetic-disease profiles. Their mother should have been vaccinated, free of all internal and external parasites and properly nourished. For these reasons, a visit to the veterinarian who cared for the dam (mother) is recommended. The dam can pass on disease resistance to her puppies, which can last for eight to ten weeks. She can also pass on parasites and many infections. That's why it is helpful to know about the dam's health.

PUPPY VACCINATIONS
Your veterinarian will probably recommend that your puppy be fully vaccinated before you take him outside. There are airborne diseases, parasite eggs in the grass and unexpected visits from other dogs that might be dangerous to your puppy's health. Other dogs are the most harmful reservoir of pathogenic organisms, as everything they have can be transmitted to your puppy.

Weaning to Bringing Pup Home
Puppies should be weaned by the time they are about two months old. A puppy that remains for at least eight weeks with his mother and littermates usually adapts better to other dogs and people later in his life.

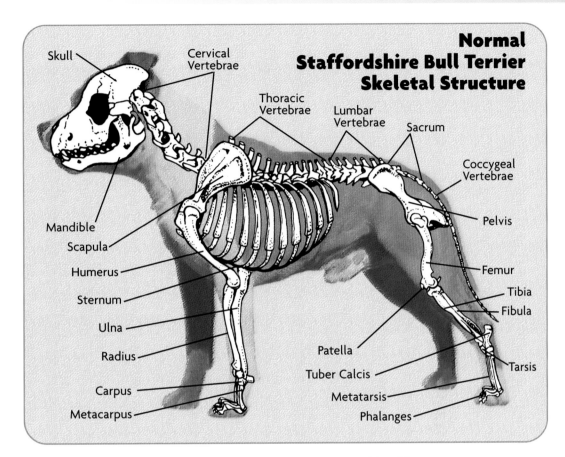

Normal Staffordshire Bull Terrier Skeletal Structure

Skull
Cervical Vertebrae
Thoracic Vertebrae
Lumbar Vertebrae
Sacrum
Coccygeal Vertebrae
Pelvis
Femur
Tibia
Fibula
Tarsis
Patella
Tuber Calcis
Metatarsis
Phalanges
Mandible
Scapula
Humerus
Sternum
Ulna
Radius
Carpus
Metacarpus

You should have your newly acquired puppy examined by a veterinarian as soon as possible after bringing him home, or even before bringing him home. The puppy will have his teeth examined and have his skeletal confor-

mation and general health checked prior to certification by the veterinarian. Many puppies have problems with their kneecaps, cataracts and other eye problems, heart murmurs and undescended testicles. Your vet

MORE THAN VACCINES

Vaccinations help prevent your new puppy from contracting diseases, but they do not cure them. Proper nutrition as well as parasite control keep your dog healthy and less susceptible to many dangerous diseases. Remember that your dog depends on you to ensure his well-being.

might also have training in temperament evaluation. At the first visit, the veterinarian will set up a schedule for the pup's vaccinations.

VACCINATION SCHEDULING

Most vaccinations are given by injection and should only be done by a veterinarian. Both he and you should keep a record of the date of the injection, the identification of the vaccine and the amount given. The first vaccinations should start when the puppy is 6–8 weeks of age, the second when he is 10–12 weeks of age and the third when he is 14–16 weeks of age. Vaccinations are usually based on a two- to four-week schedule.

Most vaccinations immunize your puppy against viruses. The usual vaccines contain immunizing doses of several different viruses such as distemper, parvovirus, parainfluenza and hepatitis. There are other vaccines available when the puppy is at risk. You should rely upon professional advice. This is especially true for the booster-shot program. Most vaccination programs require a booster when the puppy

DISEASE REFERENCE CHART

	What is it?	What causes it?	Symptoms
Leptospirosis	Severe disease that affects the internal organs; can be spread to people.	A bacterium, which is often carried by rodents, that enters through mucous membranes and spreads quickly throughout the body.	Range from fever, vomiting and loss of appetite in less severe cases to shock, irreversible kidney damage and possibly death in most severe cases.
Rabies	Potentially deadly virus that infects warm-blooded mammals.	Bite from a carrier of the virus, mainly wild animals.	1st stage: dog exhibits change in behavior, fear. 2nd stage: dog's behavior becomes more aggressive. 3rd stage: loss of coordination, trouble with bodily functions.
Parvovirus	Highly contagious virus, potentially deadly.	Ingestion of the virus, which is usually spread through the feces of infected dogs.	Most common: severe diarrhea. Also vomiting, fatigue, lack of appetite.
Canine cough	Contagious respiratory infection.	Combination of types of bacteria and virus. Most common: *Bordetella bronchiseptica* bacteria and parainfluenza virus.	Chronic cough.
Distemper	Disease primarily affecting respiratory and nervous system.	Virus that is related to the human measles virus.	Mild symptoms such as fever, lack of appetite and mucus secretion progress to evidence of brain damage, "hard pad."
Hepatitis	Virus primarily affecting the liver.	Canine adenovirus type I (CAV-1). Enters system when dog breathes in particles.	Lesser symptoms include listlessness, diarrhea, vomiting. More severe symptoms include "blue-eye" (clumps of virus in eye).
Coronavirus	Virus resulting in digestive problems.	Virus is spread through infected dog's feces.	Stomach upset evidenced by lack of appetite, vomiting, diarrhea.

HEALTH AND VACCINATION SCHEDULE

Age in Weeks:	6th	8th	10th	12th	14th	16th	20-24th	52nd
Worm Control	✔	✔	✔	✔	✔	✔	✔	
Neutering							✔	
Heartworm		✔		✔		✔	✔	
Parvovirus	✔		✔		✔		✔	✔
Distemper		✔		✔		✔		✔
Hepatitis		✔		✔		✔		✔
Leptospirosis								✔
Parainfluenza	✔		✔		✔			✔
Dental Examination		✔					✔	✔
Complete Physical		✔					✔	✔
Coronavirus				✔			✔	✔
Canine Cough	✔							
Hip Dysplasia							✔	
Rabies							✔	

Vaccinations are not instantly effective. It takes about two weeks for the dog's immune system to develop antibodies. Most vaccinations require annual booster shots. Your vet should guide you in this regard.

is a year old, and once a year thereafter. In some cases, circumstances may require more or less frequent immunizations.

Canine cough, more formally known as tracheobronchitis, is treated with a vaccine which is sprayed into the dog's nostrils. This is often given as part of routine vaccinations, but may not be as effective as the vaccines for the other major diseases.

FIVE MONTHS TO ONE YEAR OF AGE
By the time your puppy is five months old, he should have completed his vaccination program. During his physical examination, he should be evaluated for the common hip dysplasia and other diseases of the joints. There are tests to assist in the prediction of these problems. Other tests can be run to assess the effectiveness of the vaccination program.

Unless you intend to breed or show your dog, neutering the puppy at around six months of age is recommended. Discuss this with your veterinarian. Most professionals advise neutering,

VACCINE ALLERGIES
Vaccines do not work all the time. Sometimes dogs are allergic to them and many times the antibodies, which are supposed to be stimulated by the vaccine, just are not produced. You should keep your dog in the veterinary clinic for an hour after he is vaccinated to be sure there are no allergic reactions.

and many breeders require new owners to agree to neuter pet-only puppies at the appropriate age. Neutering/spaying has proven to be extremely beneficial to both male and female dogs. Besides eliminating the possibility of pregnancy and pyometra in bitches and testicular cancer in males, it greatly reduces the risk of breast cancer in bitches and prostate cancer in males.

DOGS OLDER THAN ONE YEAR
Continue to visit the veterinarian at least once a year. There is no such disease as old age, but bodily functions do change with age. The eyes and ears are no longer as efficient. Liver, kidney and intestine functions often decline. Proper dietary changes, recommended by your veterinarian, can make life more pleasant for the aging Stafford and you.

SKIN PROBLEMS IN STAFFORDS
Veterinarians are consulted by dog owners for skin problems more than for any other group of diseases or maladies. Dogs' skin is almost as sensitive as human skin and both can suffer from almost the same ailments (though the occurrence of acne in most breeds is rare). For this reason, veterinary dermatology has developed into a specialty practiced by many veterinarians.

Since many skin problems have visual symptoms which are almost identical, it requires the skill of an experienced veterinary dermatologist to identify and cure many of the more severe skin disorders. Pet shops sell many treatments for skin problems, but most of the treatments are directed at symptoms and not the underlying problem(s). If your dog is suffering from a skin disorder, you should seek professional assistance as quickly as possible. As with all diseases, the earlier a problem is identified and treated, the more likely it is that the cure will be successful.

HEREDITARY SKIN DISORDERS
Veterinary dermatologists are currently researching a number of skin disorders that are believed to have a hereditary basis. These inherited diseases are transmitted by both parents, who appear (phenotypically) normal but have a

recessive gene for the disease, meaning that they carry, but are not affected by, the disease. These diseases pose serious problems to breeders because in some instances there are no methods of identifying carriers. Often the secondary diseases associated with these skin conditions are even more debilitating than the skin disorders themselves, including cancers and respiratory problems.

Among the hereditary skin disorders, for which the mode of inheritance is known, are cutaneous asthenia (Ehlers-Danlos syndrome), sebaceous adenitis, cyclic hematopoiesis, dermatomyositis, IgA deficiency, color dilution alopecia and nodular dermatofibrosis. All inherited diseases must be diagnosed and treated by a veterinary specialist.

PARASITE BITES

Many of us are allergic to mosquito bites. The bites itch, erupt and may even become infected. Dogs have the same reaction to fleas, ticks and/or mites. When you feel the prick of the mosquito as it bites you, you have a chance to kill it with your hand. Unfortunately, when your dog is bitten by a flea, tick or mite, he can only scratch it away or bite it. By the time the dog has been bitten, the parasite has done some of its damage. It may also have laid eggs to cause further problems in the near future. The itch-

ROUTINE CARE

A dental examination is in order when the dog is between six months and one year of age so that any permanent teeth that have erupted incorrectly can be corrected. It is important to begin a brushing regimen at home, using dental-care products made for dogs, such as doggy toothbrushes and specially formulated canine toothpaste. Durable nylon and safe edible chews should be a part of your dog's arsenal for good health, good teeth and pleasant breath. The vast majority of dogs three to four years old and older has diseases of their gums from lack of dental attention. Using the various types of dental chews can be very effective in controlling dental plaque.

By the time your dog is a year old, you should have become very comfortable with your chosen veterinarian and have agreed on scheduled visits for check-ups and booster vaccinations. Blood tests should be taken regularly, for comparative purposes for such variables as cholesterol and triglyceride levels, thyroid hormones, liver enzymes, blood cell counts, etc.

The eyes, ears, nose and throat should be examined regularly, and teeth should be cleaned by the vet once a year. For teeth scaling, it often is necessary for the dog to be anesthetized.

ing from parasite bites is probably due to the saliva injected into the site when the parasite sucks the dog's blood.

ACRAL LICK GRANULOMA

Staffords and other dogs about the same size have a very poorly understood syndrome called acral lick granuloma. The manifestation of the problem is the dog's tireless attack at a specific area of the body, almost always the legs. The dog licks so intensively that he removes the hair and skin, leaving an ugly, large wound. There is no absolute cure, but corticosteroids are the most common treatment.

AUTO-IMMUNE SKIN CONDITIONS

Auto-immune skin conditions are commonly referred to as being allergic to yourself, although allergies are usually inflammatory reactions to an outside stimulus. Auto-immune diseases cause seri-ous damage to the tissues that are involved.

The best known auto-immune disease is lupus, which affects people as well as dogs. The symptoms are variable and may affect the kidneys, bones, blood chemistry and skin. It can be fatal to both dogs and humans, though it is not thought to be transmissible. It is usually successfully treated with cortisone, prednisone or similar corticosteroid, but extensive use of these drugs can have harmful side effects.

AIRBORNE ALLERGIES

Just as humans have hay fever, rose fever and other fevers with which they suffer during the pollinating season, many dogs suffer from the same allergies. When the pollen count is high, dogs might suffer, but do not expect them to sneeze and have runny noses like humans. Dogs react to pollen allergies the same way they react to fleas—they scratch and bite themselves. Staffords can be very susceptible to airborne pollen allergies.

Dogs, like humans, can be tested for allergens. Discuss the testing with your veterinary dermatologist.

FOOD PROBLEMS

FOOD ALLERGIES

Dogs can be allergic to many foods that are best-sellers and highly

---

"P" STANDS FOR PROBLEM

Urinary tract disease is a serious condition that requires immediate medical attention. Symptoms include urinating in inappropriate places or the need to urinate frequently in small amounts. Urinary tract disease is most effectively treated with antibiotics. To help promote good urinary tract health, owners must always be sure that a constant supply of fresh water is available to their pets.

recommended by breeders and veterinarians. Changing the brand of food that you buy may not eliminate the problem if the element to which the dog is allergic is contained in the new brand.

Recognizing a food allergy is difficult. Humans vomit or have rashes when they eat a food to which they are allergic. Dogs neither vomit nor (usually) develop rashes. They react in the same manner as they do to an airborne or flea allergy: they itch, scratch and bite, thus making the diagnosis extremely difficult. While pollen allergies and parasite bites are usually seasonal, food allergies are year-round problems.

TREATING FOOD PROBLEMS

Handling food allergies and food intolerance yourself is possible. Put your dog on a diet that he has never had. Obviously, if he has never eaten this new food, he can't have been allergic or intolerant of it. Start with a single ingredient that is *not* in the dog's diet at the present time. Ingredients like chopped beef or chicken are common in dog's diets, so try something else like fish, lamb or some other quality protein source. Keep the dog on this diet (with no additives) for a month. If the symptoms of food allergy or intolerance disappear, chances are your dog has a food allergy.

Don't think that the single ingredient cured the problem. You

FOOD INTOLERANCE

Food intolerance is the inability of the dog to completely digest certain foods. For example, puppies that may have done very well on their mother's milk may not do well on cow's milk. The result of this food intolerance may be loose bowels, passing gas and stomach pains. These are the only obvious symptoms of food intolerance, and that makes diagnosis difficult.

still must find a suitable diet and ascertain which ingredient in the old diet was objectionable. This is most easily done by adding ingredients to the new diet one at a time. Let the dog stay on the modified diet for a month before you add another ingredient. Eventually, you will determine the ingredient that caused the adverse reaction.

An alternative method is to carefully study the ingredients in the diet to which your dog is allergic or intolerable. Identify the main ingredient in this diet and eliminate the main ingredient by buying a different food which does not have that ingredient. Keep experimenting until the symptoms disappear after one month on the new diet.

A male dog flea, *Ctenocephalides canis*.

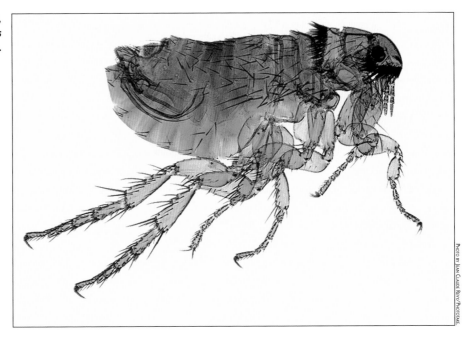

Photo by Jean Claude Revy/Phototake

EXTERNAL PARASITES

FLEAS

Of all the problems to which dogs are prone, none is more well known and frustrating than fleas. Flea infestation is relatively simple to cure but difficult to prevent. Parasites that are harbored inside the body are a bit more difficult to eradicate but they are easier to control.

To control flea infestation, you have to understand the flea's life cycle. Fleas are often thought of as a summertime problem, but centrally heated homes have changed the patterns and fleas can be found at any time of the year. The most effective method of flea control is a two-stage approach: one stage to kill the adult fleas, and the other to control the development of pre-adult fleas. Unfortunately, no single active ingredient is effective against all stages of the life cycle.

FLEA KILLER CAUTION— "POISON"

Flea-killers are poisonous. You should not spray these toxic chemicals on areas of a dog's body that he licks, including his genitals and his face. Flea killers taken internally are a better answer, but check with your vet in case internal therapy is not advised for your dog.

LIFE CYCLE STAGES

During its life, a flea will pass through four life stages: egg, larva, pupa or nymph and adult. The adult stage is the most visible and irritating stage of the flea life cycle, and this is why the majority of flea-control products concentrate on this stage. The fact is that adult fleas account for only 1% of the total flea population, and the other 99% exist in pre-adult stages, i.e. eggs, larvae and nymphs. The pre-adult stages are barely visible to the naked eye.

THE LIFE CYCLE OF THE FLEA

Eggs are laid on the dog, usually in quantities of about 20 or 30, several times a day. The adult female flea must have a blood meal before each egg-laying session. When first laid, the eggs will cling to the dog's hair, as the eggs are still moist. However, they will quickly dry out and fall from the dog, especially if the dog moves around or scratches. Many eggs will fall off in the dog's favorite area or an area in which he spends a lot of time, such as his bed.

Once the eggs fall from the dog onto the carpet or furniture, they will hatch into larvae. This takes from one to ten days. Larvae are not particularly mobile and will usually travel only a few inches from where they hatch. However, they do have a tendency to move away from bright light and heavy

EN GARDE:
CATCHING FLEAS OFF GUARD!
Consider the following ways to arm yourself against fleas:

- Add a small amount of pennyroyal or eucalyptus oil to your dog's bath. These natural remedies repel fleas.
- Supplement your dog's food with fresh garlic (minced or grated) and a hearty amount of brewer's yeast, both of which ward off fleas.
- Use a flea comb on your dog daily. Submerge fleas in a cup of bleach to kill them quickly.
- Confine the dog to only a few rooms to limit the spread of fleas in the home.
- Vacuum daily...and get all of the crevices! Dispose of the bag every few days until the problem is under control.
- Wash your dog's bedding daily. Cover cushions where your dog sleeps with towels, and wash the towels often.

traffic—under furniture and behind doors are common places to find high quantities of flea larvae.

The flea larvae feed on dead organic matter, including adult flea feces, until they are ready to change into adult fleas. Fleas will usually remain as larvae for around seven days. After this period, the larvae will pupate into protective pupae. While inside the pupae, the larvae will undergo metamorphosis and change into adult fleas. This can take as little time as a few days, but the adult fleas can remain inside the pupae waiting to hatch for up to two years. The pupae are signaled to hatch by certain stimuli, such as physical pressure—the pupae's being stepped on, heat from an animal's lying on the pupae or increased carbon-dioxide levels and vibrations—indicating that a suitable host is available.

Once hatched, the adult flea must feed within a few days. Once the adult flea finds a host, it will not leave voluntarily. It only becomes dislodged by grooming or the host animal's scratching. The adult flea will remain on the

PHOTO BY DWIGHT R. KUHN.

host for the duration of its life unless forcibly removed.

TREATING THE ENVIRONMENT AND THE DOG

Treating fleas should be a two-pronged attack. First, the environment needs to be treated; this includes carpets and furniture, especially the dog's bedding and areas underneath furniture. The environment should be treated with a household spray containing an Insect Growth Regulator (IGR) and an insecticide to kill the adult fleas. Most IGRs are effective against eggs and larvae; they actually mimic the fleas' own hormones and stop the eggs and larvae from developing into adult fleas. There are currently no treatments available to attack the pupa stage of the life cycle, so the adult insecticide is used to kill the newly hatched adult fleas before they find a host. Most IGRs are active for many months, while adult insecticides are only active for a few days.

A scanning electron micrograph of a dog or cat flea, *Ctenocephalides*, magnified more than 100x. This image has been colorized for effect.

S. E. M. BY DR. DENNIS KUNKEL, UNIVERSITY OF HAWAII.

THE LIFE CYCLE OF THE FLEA

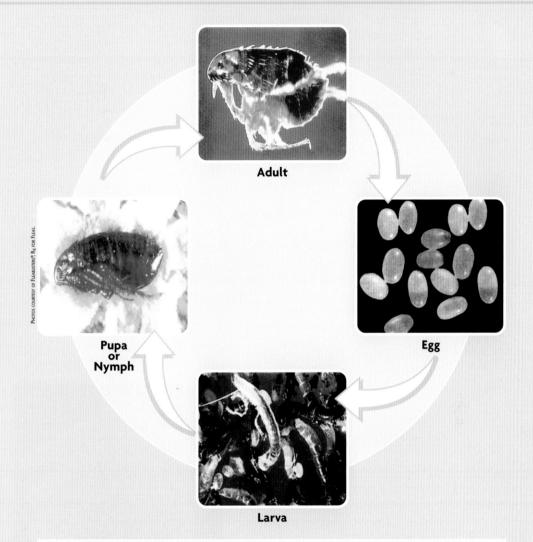

Adult

Egg

Larva

Pupa
or
Nymph

A LOOK AT FLEAS

Fleas have been around for millions of years and have adapted to changing host animals. They are able to go through a complete life cycle in less than one month or they can extend their lives to almost two years by remaining as pupae or cocoons. They do not need blood or any other food for up to 20 months.

> ## INSECT GROWTH REGULATOR (IGR)
>
> Two types of products should be used when treating fleas—a product to treat the pet and a product to treat the home. Adult fleas represent less than 1% of the flea population. The pre-adult fleas (eggs, larvae and pupae) represent more than 99% of the flea population and are found in the environment; it is in the case of pre-adult fleas that products containing an Insect Growth Regulator (IGR) should be used in the home.
>
> IGRs are a new class of compounds used to prevent the development of insects. They do not kill the insect outright, but instead use the insect's biology against it to stop it from completing its growth. Products that contain methoprene are the world's first and leading IGRs. Used to control fleas and other insects, this type of IGR will stop flea larvae from developing and protect the house for up to seven months.

The American dog tick, *Dermacentor variabilis*, is probably the most common tick found on dogs. Look at the strength in its eight legs! No wonder it's hard to detach them.

When treating with a household spray, it is a good idea to vacuum before applying the product. This stimulates as many pupae as possible to hatch into adult fleas. The vacuum cleaner should also be treated with an insecticide to prevent the eggs and larvae that have been collected in the vacuum bag from hatching.

The second stage of treatment is to apply an adult insecticide to the dog. Traditionally, this would be in the form of a collar or a spray, but more recent innovations include digestible insecticides that poison the fleas when they ingest the dog's blood. Alternatively, there are drops that, when placed on the back of the dog's neck, spread throughout the hair and skin to kill adult fleas.

TICKS

Though not as common as fleas, ticks are found all over the tropical and temperate world. They don't bite, like fleas; they harpoon. They dig their sharp proboscis (nose) into the dog's skin and drink the blood. Their only food and drink is dog's

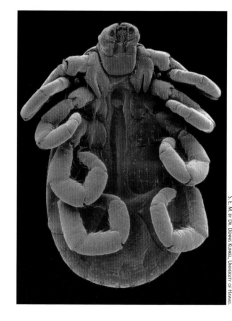

S.E.M. BY DR. DENNIS KUNKEL, UNIVERSITY OF HAWAII

blood. Dogs can get Lyme disease, Rocky Mountain spotted fever, tick bite paralysis and many other diseases from ticks. They may live where fleas are found and they like to hide in cracks or seams in walls. They are controlled the same way fleas are controlled.

The American dog tick, *Dermacentor variabilis*, may well be the most common dog tick in many geographical areas, especially those areas where the climate is hot and humid. Most dog ticks have life expectancies of a week to six months, depending upon climatic conditions. They can neither jump nor fly, but they can crawl slowly and can range up to 16 feet to reach a sleeping or unsuspecting dog.

MITES

Just as fleas and ticks can be problematic for your dog, mites can also lead to an itchy nuisance. Microscopic in size, mites are related to ticks and generally take up permanent residence on their host animal—in this case, your dog! The term *mange* refers to any infestation caused by one of the mighty mites, of which there are six varieties that concern dog owners.

Demodex mites cause a condition known as demodicosis (sometimes called red mange or

DEER-TICK CROSSING

The great outdoors may be fun for your dog, but it also is an home to dangerous ticks. Deer ticks carry a bacterium known as *Borrelia burgdorferi* and are most active in the autumn and spring. When infections are caught early, penicillin and tetracycline are effective antibiotics, but, if left untreated, the bacteria may cause neurological, kidney and cardiac problems as well as long-term trouble with walking and painful joints.

S.E.M. BY DR. ANDREW SPIELMAN/PHOTOTAKE.

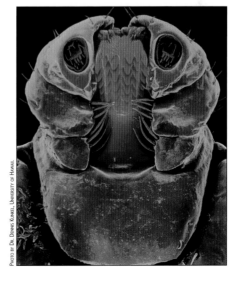

PHOTO BY DR. DENNIS KUNKEL, UNIVERSITY OF HAWAII.

The head of an American dog tick, *Dermacentor variabilis*, enlarged and colorized for effect.

The mange mite, *Psoroptes bovis*, can infest cattle and other domestic animals.

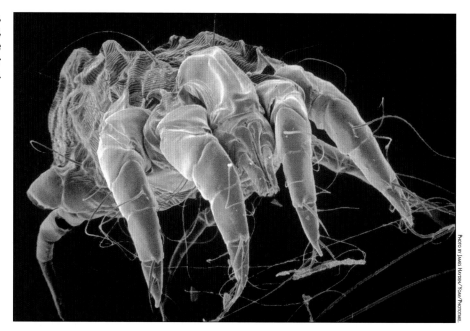

PHOTO BY JAMES HAYDEN/YOAV/PHOTOTAKE.

follicular mange), in which the mites live in the dog's hair follicles and sebaceous glands in larger-than-normal amounts.

This type of mange is commonly passed from the dam to her puppies and usually shows up on the puppies' muzzles, though demodicosis is not transferable from one normal dog to another. Most dogs recover from this type of mange without any treatment, though topical therapies are commonly prescribed by the vet.

The *Cheyletiellosis* mite is the hook-mouthed culprit associated with "walking dandruff," a condition that affects dogs as well as cats and rabbits. This mite lives on the surface of the animal's skin and is readily transferable through direct or indirect contact with an affected animal. The dandruff is present in the form of scaly skin, which may or may not be itchy. If not treated, this mange can affect a whole kennel of dogs and can be spread to humans as well.

The *Sarcoptes* mite causes intense itching on the dog in the form of a condition known as scabies or sarcoptic mange. The cycle of the *Sarcoptes* mite lasts about three weeks, and the mites live in the top layer of the dog's skin (epidermis), preferably in

Human lice look like dog lice; the two are closely related.

PHOTO BY DWIGHT R. KUHN.

areas with little hair. Scabies is highly contagious and can be passed to humans. Sometimes an allergic reaction to the mite worsens the severe itching associated with sarcoptic mange.

Ear mites, *Otodectes cynotis,* lead to otodectic mange, which most commonly affects the outer ear canal of the dog, though other areas can be affected as well. Dogs with ear-mite infestation commonly scratch at their ears, causing further irritation, and shake their heads. Dark brown droppings in the outer ear confirm the diagnosis. Your vet can prescribe a treatment to flush out the ears and kill any eggs in the ears. A complete month of treatment is necessary to cure the mange.

Two other mites, less common in dogs, include *Dermanyssus gallinae* (the poultry or red mite) and *Eutrombicula alfreddugesi* (the North American mite associated with trombiculidiasis or chigger infestation). The poultry mite frequently lives on chickens, but can transfer to dogs who spend time near farm animals. Chigger infestation affects dogs in the

NOT A DROP TO DRINK

Never allow your dog to swim in polluted water or public areas where water quality can be suspect. Even perfectly clear water can harbor parasites, many of which can cause serious to fatal illnesses in canines. Areas inhabited by waterfowl and other wildlife are especially dangerous.

Central US who have exposure to woodlands. The types of mange caused by both of these mites are treatable by veterinarians.

INTERNAL PARASITES

Most animals—fishes, birds and mammals, including dogs and humans—have worms and other parasites that live inside their bodies. According to Dr. Herbert R. Axelrod, the fish pathologist, there are two kinds of parasites: dumb and smart. The smart parasites live in peaceful cooperation with their hosts (symbiosis), while the dumb parasites kill their hosts. Most worm infections are relatively easy to control. If they are not controlled, they weaken the host dog to the point that other medical problems occur, but they do not kill the host as dumb parasites would.

The brown dog tick, *Rhipicephalus sanguineus,* is an uncommon but annoying tick found on dogs.

PHOTO BY CAROLINA BIOLOGICAL SUPPLY/PHOTOTAKE.

DO NOT MIX

Never mix parasite-control products without first consulting your vet. Some products can become toxic when combined with others and can cause fatal consequences.

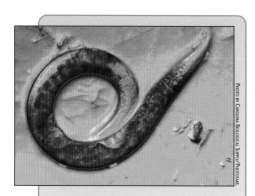

The roundworm *Rhabditis* can infect both dogs and humans.

ROUNDWORMS

Average-size dogs can pass 1,360,000 roundworm eggs every day. For example, if there were only 1 million dogs in the world, the world would be saturated with thousands of tons of dog feces. These feces would contain around 15,000,000,000 roundworm eggs.

Up to 31% of home yards and children's sand boxes in the US contain roundworm eggs.

Flushing dog's feces down the toilet is not a safe practice because the usual sewage treatments do not destroy roundworm eggs.

Infected puppies start shedding roundworm eggs at three weeks of age. They can be infected by their mother's milk.

The roundworm, *Ascaris lumbricoides*.

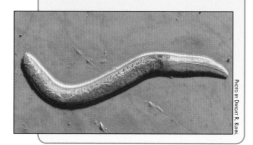

ROUNDWORMS

The roundworms that infect dogs are known scientifically as *Toxocara canis*. They live in the dog's intestines and shed eggs continually. It has been estimated that a dog produces about 6 or more ounces of feces every day. Each ounce of feces averages hundreds of thousands of roundworm eggs. There are no known areas in which dogs roam that do not contain roundworm eggs. The greatest danger of roundworms is that they infect people, too! It is wise to have your dog tested regularly for roundworms.

In young puppies, roundworms cause bloated bellies, diarrhea, coughing and vomiting, and are transmitted from the dam (through blood or milk). Affected puppies will not appear as animated as normal puppies. The worms appear spaghetti-like, measuring as long as 6 inches. Adult dogs can acquire roundworms through coprophagia (eating contaminated feces) or by killing rodents that carry roundworms.

Roundworm infection can kill puppies and cause severe problems in adults, as the hatched larvae travel to the lungs and trachea through the bloodstream. Cleanliness is the best preventative for roundworms. Always pick up after your dog and dispose of feces in appropriate receptacles.

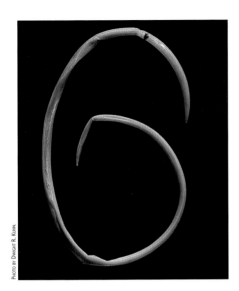

Photo by Dwight R. Kuhn.

HOOKWORMS

In the United States, dog owners have to be concerned about four different species of hookworm, the most common and most serious of which is *Ancylostoma caninum,* which prefers warm climates. The others are *Ancylostoma braziliense, Ancylostoma tubaeforme* and *Uncinaria stenocephala,* the latter of which is a concern to dogs living in the Northern US and Canada, as this species prefers cold climates. Hookworms are dangerous to humans as well as to dogs and cats, and can be the cause of severe anemia due to iron deficiency. The worm uses its teeth to attach itself to the dog's intestines and changes the site of its attachment about six times per day. Each time the worm repositions itself, the dog loses blood and can become anemic. *Ancylostoma caninum* is the most likely of the four species to cause anemia in the dog.

The hookworm, *Ancylostoma caninum.*

Symptoms of hookworm infection include dark stools, weight loss, general weakness, pale coloration and anemia, as well as possible skin problems. Fortunately, hookworms are easily purged from the affected dog with a number of medications that have proven effective. Discuss these with your veterinarian. Most heartworm preventatives include a hookworm insecticide as well.

Owners also must be aware that hookworms can infect humans, who can acquire the larvae through exposure to contaminated feces. Since the worms cannot complete their life cycle on a human, the worms simply infest the skin and cause irritation. This condition is known as cutaneous larva migrans syndrome. As a preventative, use disposable gloves or a "poop-scoop" to pick up your dog's droppings and prevent your dog (or neighborhood cats) from defecating in children's play areas.

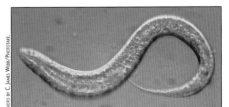

Photo by C. James Webb/Phototake.

The infective stage of the hookworm larva.

TAPEWORMS

Humans, rats, squirrels, foxes, coyotes, wolves and domestic dogs are all susceptible to tapeworm infection. Except in humans, tapeworms are usually not a fatal infection. Infected individuals can harbor 1000 parasitic worms.

Tapeworms, like some other types of worm, are hermaphroditic, meaning male and female in the same worm.

If dogs eat infected rats or mice, or anything else infected with tapeworm, they get the tapeworm disease. One month after attaching to a dog's intestine, the worm starts shedding eggs. These eggs are infective immediately. Infective eggs can live for a few months without a host animal.

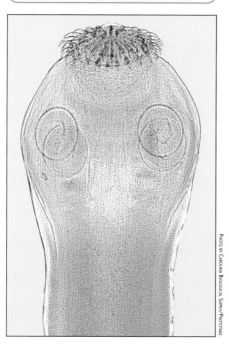

The head and rostellum (the round prominence on the scolex) of a tapeworm, which infects dogs and humans.

PHOTO BY CAROLINA BIOLOGICAL SUPPLY/PHOTOTAKE.

TAPEWORMS

There are many species of tapeworm, all of which are carried by fleas! The most common tapeworm affecting dogs is known as *Dipylidium caninum*. The dog eats the flea and starts the tapeworm cycle. Humans can also be infected with tapeworms—so don't eat fleas! Fleas are so small that your dog could pass them onto your hands, your plate or your food and thus make it possible for you to ingest a flea that is carrying tapeworm eggs.

While tapeworm infection is not life-threatening in dogs (smart parasite!), it can be the cause of a very serious liver disease for humans. About 50% of the humans infected with *Echinococcus multilocularis*, a type of tapeworm that causes alveolar hydatid, perish.

WHIPWORMS

In North America, whipworms are counted among the most common parasitic worms in dogs. The whipworm's scientific name is *Trichuris vulpis*. These worms attach themselves in the lower parts of the intestine, where they feed. Affected dogs may only experience upset tummies, colic and diarrhea. These worms, however, can live for months or years in the dog, beginning their larval stage in the small intestine, spending their adult stage in the large intestine and finally passing infective eggs through the dog's feces. The only way to detect whipworms is through a fecal examination, though this is not always foolproof. Treatment for whipworms is tricky, due to the worms' unusual life-cycle pattern, and very often dogs are reinfected due to exposure to infective eggs on the ground. The whipworm eggs can survive in the environment for as long as five years; thus, cleaning up droppings in your own backyard as well as in public places is absolutely essential for sanitation purposes and the health of your dog and others.

THREADWORMS

Though less common than round-worms, hookworms and those already mentioned, threadworms concern dog owners in the Southwestern US and Gulf Coast area where the climate is hot and humid. Living in the small intes-tine of the dog, this worm measures a mere 2 millimeters and is round in shape. Like that of the whip-worm, the threadworm's life cycle is very complex and the eggs and larvae are passed through the feces. A deadly disease in humans, *Strongyloides* readily infects people, and the handling of feces is the most common means of trans-mission. Threadworms are most often seen in young puppies; bloody diarrhea and pneumonia are symptoms. Sick puppies must be isolated and treated immediately; vets recommend a follow-up treat-ment one month later.

HEARTWORM PREVENTATIVES

There are many heartworm preventatives on the market, many of which are sold at your veterinarian's office. These products can be given daily or monthly, depending on the manufacturer's instructions. All of these preventatives contain chemical insecticides directed at killing heartworms, which leads to some controversy among dog owners. In effect, heartworm preventatives are neces-sary evils, though you should determine how necessary based on your pet's lifestyle. There is no doubt that heartworm is a dreadful disease that threatens the lives of dogs. However, the likelihood of your dog's being bitten by an infected mosquito is slim in most places, and a mosquito-repellent (or an herbal remedy such as Wormwood or Black Walnut) is much safer for your dog and will not compromise his immune system (the way heartworm preventatives will). Should you decide to use the traditional preventa-tive "medications," you can consider giving the pill every other or third month. Since the toxins in the pill will kill the heart-worms at all stages of development, the pill would be effective in killing larvae, nymphs or adults, and it takes four months for the larvae to reach the adult stage. Thus, there is no rationale to poisoning the dog's system on a monthly basis. Lastly, do not give the pill during the winter months since there are no mosquitoes around to pass on their infection, unless you live in a tropical environment.

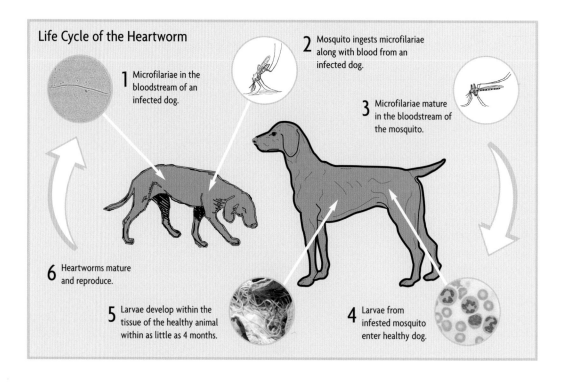

Life Cycle of the Heartworm

1 Microfilariae in the bloodstream of an infected dog.

2 Mosquito ingests microfilariae along with blood from an infected dog.

3 Microfilariae mature in the bloodstream of the mosquito.

4 Larvae from infested mosquito enter healthy dog.

5 Larvae develop within the tissue of the healthy animal within as little as 4 months.

6 Heartworms mature and reproduce.

HEARTWORMS

Heartworms are thin, extended worms up to 12 inches long, which live in a dog's heart and the major blood vessels surrounding it. Dogs may have up to 200 worms. Symptoms may be loss of energy, loss of appetite, coughing, the development of a pot belly and anemia.

Heartworms are transmitted by mosquitoes. The mosquito drinks the blood of an infected dog and takes in larvae with the blood. The larvae, called microfilariae, develop within the body of the mosquito and are passed on to the next dog bitten after the larvae mature. It takes two to three weeks for the larvae to develop to the infective stage within the body of the mosquito. Dogs are usually treated at about six weeks of age and maintained on a prophylactic dose given monthly.

Blood testing for heartworms is not necessarily indicative of how seriously your dog is infected. Although this is a dangerous disease, it is not easy for a dog to be infected. Discuss the various preventatives with your vet, as there are many different types now available. Together you can decide on a safe course of prevention for your dog.

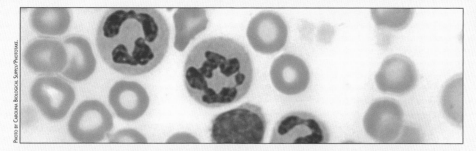

Magnified heart-worm larvae, *Dirofilaria immitis.*

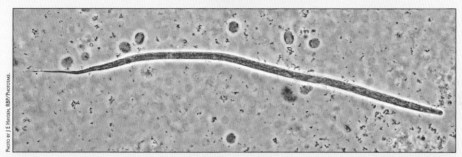

Heartworm, *Dirofilaria immitis.*

The heart of a dog infected with canine heart-worm, *Dirofilaria immitis.*

CDS: COGNITIVE DYSFUNCTION SYNDROME
"Old-Dog Syndrome"

There are many ways for you to evaluate old-dog syndrome. Veterinarians have defined CDS (cognitive dysfunction syndrome) as the gradual deterioration of cognitive abilities. These are indicated by changes in the dog's behavior. When a dog changes his routine response, and maladies have been eliminated as the cause of these behavioral changes, then CDS is the usual diagnosis.

More than half the dogs over eight years old suffer from some form of CDS. The older the dog, the more chance he has of suffering from CDS. In humans, doctors often dismiss the CDS behavioral changes as part of "winding down."

There are four major signs of CDS: frequent potty accidents inside the home, sleeping much more or much less than normal, acting confused and failing to respond to social stimuli.

SYMPTOMS OF CDS

FREQUENT POTTY ACCIDENTS
- *Urinates in the house.*
- *Defecates in the house.*
- *Doesn't signal that he wants to go out.*

SLEEP PATTERNS
- *Awakens more slowly.*
- *Sleeps more than normal during the day.*
- *Sleeps less during the night.*

CONFUSION
- *Goes outside and just stands there.*
- *Appears confused with a faraway look in his eyes.*
- *Hides more often.*
- *Doesn't recognize friends.*
- *Doesn't come when called.*
- *Walks around listlessly and without a destination.*

FAILURE TO RESPOND TO SOCIAL STIMULI
- *Comes to people less frequently, whether called or not.*
- *Doesn't tolerate petting for more than a short time.*
- *Doesn't come to the door when you return home.*

The term *old* is a qualitative term. For dogs, as well as their masters, old is relative. Certainly we can all distinguish between a puppy Stafford and an adult Stafford—there are the obvious physical traits, such as size, appearance and facial expressions, as well as personality traits. Puppies and young dogs like to play with children. Children's natural exuberance is a good match for the seemingly endless energy of young dogs.

As Staffords become older, the hair around their mouths turns gray. This is usually the first sign of a dog's aging.

GETTING OLD

The bottom line is simply that your dog is getting old when you think he is getting old because he slows down in his general activities, including walking, running, eating, jumping and retrieving. On the other hand, certain activities increase, like more sleeping, more barking and more repetition of habits like going to the door when you put your coat on without being called.

They like to run, jump, chase and retrieve. When dogs grow up and cease their interaction with children, they are often thought of as being too old to play with the kids.

On the other hand, if a Stafford is only exposed to people with quieter lifestyles, his life will normally be less active and the decrease in his activity level as he ages will not be as obvious.

If people live to be 100 years old, dogs live to be 20 years old. While this may sound like a viable rule of thumb, it is *very* inaccurate. When trying to

SIGNS OF AGING

An old dog starts to show one or more of the following symptoms:

- Sleep patterns are deeper and longer and the old dog is harder to awaken.

- Food intake diminishes.

- Responses to calls, whistles and other signals are ignored more and more.

- Eye contacts do not evoke tail wagging (assuming they once did).

- The hair on his face and paws starts to turn gray. The color breakdown usually starts around the eyes and mouth.

the Stafford's bull and mastiff cousins that scarcely live past 8 or 9 years.

Dogs are generally considered mature within three years, but they can reproduce even earlier. So it is more accurate to compare the first three years of a dog's life to seven times that of comparable humans. That means a three 3-year-old dog is like a 21-year-old person. As the curve of comparison shows, however, there is no hard and fast rule for comparing dog and human ages. The comparison is made even more difficult, for not all humans age at the same rate.

compare dog years to human years, you cannot make a generalization about all dogs. You can make the generalization that 13 years is a good lifespan for a Stafford, compared to some of

WHAT TO LOOK FOR IN SENIORS

Most veterinarians and behaviorists use the seven-year mark as the time to consider a dog a *senior*. This term does not imply

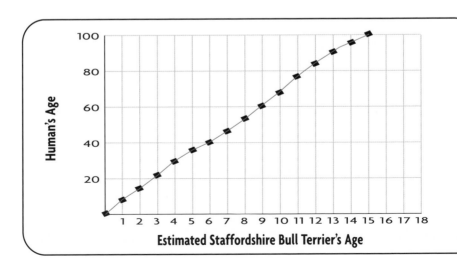

that the dog is geriatric and has begun to fail in mind and body. Aging is essentially a slowing process. Humans readily admit that they feel a difference in their activity level from age 20 to 30, and then from 30 to 40, etc. By treating the seven-year-old dog as a senior, owners are able to implement certain therapeutic and preventive medical strategies with the help of their vets.

A senior-care program should include at least two veterinary visits per year and screening sessions to determine the dog's health status, as well as nutritional counseling. Veterinarians determine the senior dog's health status through a blood smear for a complete blood count, serum chemistry profile with electrolytes, urinalysis, blood pressure check, electrocardiogram, ocular tonometry (pressure on the eyeball) and dental prophylaxis.

Such an extensive program for senior dogs is well advised before owners start to see the obvious physical signs of aging, such as slower and inhibited movement, graying, increased sleep/nap periods and disinterest in play and other activity. This preventative program promises a longer, healthier life for the aging dog. Among the physical problems common in aging dogs are the loss of sight and hearing, arthritis, kidney and liver failure,

NOTICING THE SYMPTOMS
The symptoms listed below are symptoms that gradually appear and become more noticeable. They are not life-threatening; however, the symptoms below are to be taken very seriously and warrant a discussion with your veterinarian:
• Your dog cries and whimpers when he moves, and he stops running completely.
• Convulsions start or become more serious and frequent. The usual convulsion (spasm) is when the dog stiffens and starts to tremble, being unable or unwilling to move. The seizure usually lasts for 5 to 30 minutes.
• Your dog drinks more water and urinates more frequently. Wetting and bowel accidents take place indoors without warning.
• Vomiting becomes more and more frequent.

diabetes mellitus, heart disease and Cushing's disease (a hormonal disease).

In addition to the physical manifestations discussed, there are some behavioral changes and problems related to aging dogs. Dogs suffering from hearing or vision loss, dental discomfort or arthritis can become aggressive. Likewise, the near-deaf and/or blind dog may be startled more easily and react in an unexpectedly aggressive manner. Seniors

SENIORS AND FOOD

Your senior dog may lose interest in eating, not because he's less hungry but because his senses of smell and taste have diminished. The old chow simply does not smell as good as it once did. Additionally, older dogs use less energy and thereby can sustain themselves on less food.

suffering from senility can become more impatient and irritable. Housesoiling accidents are associated with loss of mobility, kidney problems and loss of sphincter control as well as plaque accumulation, physiological brain changes and reactions to medications. Older dogs, just like young puppies, can suffer from separation anxiety, which can lead to excessive barking, whining, housesoiling and destructive behavior. Seniors may become fearful of everyday sounds, such as vacuum cleaners, heaters, thunder and passing traffic. Some dogs have difficulty sleeping, due to discomfort, the need for frequent potty visits and the like.

Owners should avoid spoiling the older dog with too many treats. Obesity is a common prob-lem in older dogs and subtracts years from their lives. Keep the senior dog as trim as possible since excess weight puts additional stress on the body's vital organs. Some breeders recommend supplementing the diet with foods high in fiber and lower in calories. Adding fresh vegetables and marrow broth to the senior's diet makes a tasty, low-calorie, low-fat supplement. Vets also offer specialty diets for senior dogs that are worth exploring.

Your dog, as he nears his twilight years, needs your patience and good care more than ever. Never punish an older dog for an accident or abnormal behavior. For all the years of love, protection and companionship that your dog has provided, he deserves special attention and courtesies. The older dog may need to relieve himself at 3 a.m. because he can no longer "hold it" for eight hours. Older dogs may not be able to remain crated for more than two or three hours. It may be time to give up a sofa or chair to your old friend. Although he may not seem as enthusiastic about your attention and petting, he does appreciate the considerations you offer as he gets older.

Your Staffordshire Bull Terrier does not understand why his world is slowing down. Owners must make their dogs'

Number-One Killer Disease in Dogs: CANCER

In every age, there is a word associated with a disease or plague that causes humans to shudder. In the 21st century, that word is "cancer." Just as cancer is the leading cause of death in humans, it claims nearly half the lives of dogs that die from a natural disease as well as half the dogs that die over the age of ten years.

Described as a genetic disease, cancer becomes a greater risk as the dog ages. Vets and dog owners have become increasingly aware of the threat of cancer to dogs. Statistics reveal that one dog in every five will develop cancer, the most common of which is skin cancer. Many cancers, including prostate, ovarian and breast cancer, can be avoided by spaying and neutering our dogs around the age of six months.

Early detection of cancer can save or extend a dog's life, so it is absolutely vital for owners to have their dogs examined by a qualified vet or oncologist immediately upon detection of any abnormality. Certain dietary guidelines have also proven to reduce the onset and spread of cancer. Foods based on fish rather than beef, due to the presence of Omega-3 fatty acids, are recommended. Other amino acids such as glutamine have significant benefits for canines, particularly those breeds that show a greater susceptibility to cancer.

Cancer management and treatments promise hope for future generations of canines. Since the disease is genetic, breeders should never breed a dog whose parents, grandparents and any related siblings have developed cancer. It is difficult to know whether to exclude an otherwise healthy dog from a breeding program as the disease does not manifest itself until the dog's senior years.

RECOGNIZE CANCER WARNING SIGNS

Since early detection can possibly rescue your dog from becoming a cancer statistic, it is essential for owners to recognize the possible signs and seek the assistance of a qualified professional.

- Abnormal bumps or lumps that continue to grow
- Bleeding or discharge from any body cavity
- Persistent stiffness or lameness
- Recurrent sores or sores that do not heal
- Inappetence
- Breathing difficulties
- Weight loss
- Bad breath or odors
- General malaise and fatigue
- Eating and swallowing problems
- Difficulty urinating and defecating

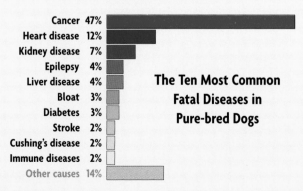

Disease	%
Cancer	47%
Heart disease	12%
Kidney disease	7%
Epilepsy	4%
Liver disease	4%
Bloat	3%
Diabetes	3%
Stroke	2%
Cushing's disease	2%
Immune diseases	2%
Other causes	14%

The Ten Most Common Fatal Diseases in Pure-bred Dogs

AN ANCIENT ACHE

As ancient a disease as any, arthritis remains poorly explained for human and dog alike. Fossils dating back 100 million years show the deterioration caused by arthritis. Human fossils two million years old show the disease in man. The most common type of arthritis affecting dogs is known as osteoarthritis, which occurs in adult dogs before their senior years. Obesity aggravating the dog's joints has been cited as a factor in arthritis.

Rheumatoid disease destroys joint cartilage and causes arthritic joints. Pituitary dysfunctions as well as diabetes have been associated with arthritis. Veterinarians treat arthritis variously, including aspirin, "bed rest" in the dog's crate, physical therapy and exercise, heat therapy (with a heating pad), soft bedding materials and treatment with corticosteroids (to reduce pain and swelling temporarily). Your vet will be able to recommend a course of action to help relieve your arthritic pal. Inquire about new drug therapies as well.

transition into the golden years as pleasant and rewarding as possible.

WHAT TO DO WHEN THE TIME COMES

You are never fully prepared to make a rational decision about putting your dog to sleep. It is very obvious that you love your Stafford or you would not be reading this book. Putting a loved dog to sleep is extremely difficult. It is a decision that must be made with your veterinarian. You are usually forced to make the decision when your dog experiences one or more life-threatening symptoms, requiring you to seek veterinary help.

If the prognosis of the malady indicates the end is near and your beloved pet will only suffer more and experience no enjoyment for the balance of his life, then euthanasia is the right choice.

WHAT IS EUTHANASIA?

Euthanasia derives from the Greek, meaning *good death*. In other words, it means the planned, painless killing of a dog suffering from a painful, incurable condition, or who is so aged that he cannot walk, see, eat or control his excretory functions.

Euthanasia is usually accomplished by injection with an overdose of an anesthesia or barbiturate. Aside from the prick of the needle, the experience is painless.

MAKING THE DECISION

The decision to euthanize your dog is hard. The days during which the dog becomes ill and the end occurs can be unusually stressful for you. If this is your first experience with the death of a loved one, you may need the comfort dictated by your religious beliefs. If you are the head of the family and have children, you should have involved them in the decision of putting your Stafford to sleep. Usually your dog can be maintained on drugs for a few days in the vet's clinic in order to give you ample time to make a decision. During this time, talking with members of the family or religious representatives, or even people who have lived through this same experience, can ease the burden of your inevitable decision. In any case, euthanasia is painful and stressful for the family of the dog.

THE FINAL RESTING PLACE

Dogs can have some of the same privileges as humans. If your dog has died at home, you can bury him in a special spot in the yard, marked by a stone or a newly planted tree or bush. Your beloved dog can be buried in a pet cemetery, which is generally expensive. Alternatively, your dog can be cremated individually and the ashes returned to you. A less expensive option is mass cremation, although, of course, the ashes of individual dogs cannot then be returned. Some owners prefer to leave their dogs at the vet's clinic.

Vets can usually help you locate a pet cemetery or arrange a cremation on your behalf. The

> **EUTHANASIA SERVICES**
> Euthanasia must be done by a licensed vet, who may be considerate enough to come to your home. There also may be societies for the prevention of cruelty to animals in your area. They often offer this service upon a vet's recommendation.

cost of these options should always be discussed frankly and openly with your vet.

GETTING ANOTHER DOG?

The grief of losing your beloved dog will be as lasting as the grief of losing a human friend or relative. In most cases, if your dog died of old age (if there is such a thing), he had slowed down considerably. Do you want a new Staffordshire Bull Terrier puppy? Or are you better off in finding a more mature Stafford, say two to three years of age, which will usually be house-trained and will have an already developed personality. In this case, you can

Pet cemeteries often have areas in which to store urns that contain dogs' ashes.

If you are interested in burying your dog, there are pet cemeteries that cater to pet lovers.

find out if you like each other after a few hours of being together.

The decision is, of course, your own. Do you want another Stafford? Perhaps you want a smaller or larger dog? How much do you want to spend on a dog? Do you want a different breed to avoid comparison with your old friend?

Most people usually stay with the same breed because they know (and love) the characteristics of that breed. Then, too, they often know people who have the same breed and perhaps they are lucky enough that a breeder whom they know and respect expects a litter soon. What could be better?

TALK IT OUT

The more openly your family discusses the whole stressful occurrence of the aging and eventual loss of a beloved pet, the easier it will be for you when the time comes.

STAFFORDSHIRE BULL TERRIER

When you purchase your Staffordshire Bull Terrier, you will make it clear to the breeder whether you want one just as a loveable companion and pet, or if you hope to be buying a Stafford with show prospects. No reputable breeder will sell you a

Staffordshire Bull Terriers often excel in the show ring. Their desire to please coupled with their impressive physiques and outgoing personalities make them ideal show dogs.

MEET THE AKC

The American Kennel Club is the main governing body of the dog sport in the United States. Founded in 1884, the AKC consists of 500 or more independent dog clubs plus 4,500 affiliate clubs, all of which follow the AKC rules and regulations. Additionally, the AKC maintains a registry for pure-bred dogs in the US and works to preserve the integrity of the sport and its continuation in the country. Over 1,000,000 dogs are registered each year, representing about 150 recognized breeds. There are over 15,000 competitive events held annually for which over 2,000,000 dogs enter to participate. Dogs compete to earn over 40 different titles, from Champion to Companion Dog to Master Agility Champion.

young puppy and tell you that it is *definitely* of show quality, for so much can go wrong during the early months of a puppy's development. If you plan to show, what you will hopefully have acquired is a puppy with "show potential."

To the novice, exhibiting a Staffordshire Bull Terrier in the show ring may look easy, but it takes a lot of hard work and devotion to do top winning at a show such as the prestigious Westminster Kennel Club dog show, not to mention a little luck, too!

The first concept that the canine novice learns when watching a dog show is that each dog first competes against members of

famous or popular, many dedicated enthusiasts say that a perfect specimen, as described in the standard, has never walked into a show ring, has never been bred and, to the woe of dog breeders around the globe, does not exist. Breeders attempt to get as close to this ideal as possible with every litter, but theoretically the "perfect" dog is so elusive that it is impossible. (And if the "perfect" dog were born, breeders and judges would never agree that it was indeed "perfect.")

If you are interested in exploring the world of dog showing, your best bet is to join your local breed club or the national parent club, which is the Staffordshire Bull Terrier Club, Inc. These clubs often host both regional and national specialties, shows only for Staffords, which can include conformation as well as obedience and other events. Even if you have no intention of competing with your Stafford, a specialty is like a festival for lovers of the breed who congregate to share their favorite topic: the Staffordshire Bull Terrier! Clubs also send out newsletters, and some organize training days and seminars in order that people may learn more about their chosen breed. To locate the breed club closest to you, contact the American Kennel Club, which furnishes the rules and regulations for all of these events plus general dog registra-

his own breed. Once the judge has selected the best member of each breed (Best of Breed), provided that the show is judged on a Group system, that chosen dog will compete with other dogs in his group. Finally, the dogs chosen first in each group will compete for Best in Show.

The second concept that you must understand is that the dogs are not actually compared against one another. The judge compares each dog against his breed standard, the written description of the ideal specimen that is approved by the American Kennel Club (AKC). While some early breed standards were indeed based on specific dogs that were

tion and other basic requirements of dog ownership.

In the US, the American Kennel Club offers three kinds of conformation shows: An all-breed show (for all AKC-recognized breeds), a specialty show (for one breed only, usually sponsored by the parent club) and a Group show (for all breeds in the group).

For a dog to become an AKC champion of record, the dog must accumulate 15 points at the shows from at least three different judges, including two "majors." A "major" is defined as a three-, four- or five-point win, and the number of points per win is determined by the number of dogs entered in the show on that day. Depending on the breed, the number of points that are awarded varies. More dogs are needed to rack up the points in more popular breeds, and less dogs are needed in less popular breeds.

At any dog show, only one dog and one bitch of each breed can win points. Dog showing does not offer "co-ed" classes. Dogs and bitches never compete against each other in the classes. Non-champion dogs are called "class dogs" because they compete in one of five classes. Dogs are entered in a particular class depending on age and previous show wins. To begin, there is the Puppy Class (for 6- to 9-month-olds and for 9- to 12-month-olds); this class is followed by the

Novice Class (for dogs that have not won any first prizes except in the Puppy Class or three first prizes in the Novice Class and

PRACTICE AT HOME

If you have decided to show your dog, you must train him to gait around the ring by your side at the correct pace and pattern, and to tolerate being handled and examined by the judge. Most breeds require complete dentition, all breeds require a particular bite (scissors, level or undershot) and all males must have two apparently normal testicles fully descended into the scrotum. Enlist family and friends to hold mock trials in your yard to prepare your future champion!

have not accumulated any points toward their championship); the Bred-by Exhibitor Class (for dogs handled by their breeders or by one of the breeder's immediate family); the American-bred Class (for dogs bred in the US); and the Open Class (for any dog that is not a champion).

The judge at the show begins judging the Puppy Class, first dogs and then bitches, and proceeds through the classes. The judge places his winners first through fourth in each class. In the Winners Class, the first-place winners of each class compete with one another to determine Winners Dog and Winners Bitch. The judge also places a Reserve

The show lead, used in the ring, is much thinner than the leads used for everyday walks and training.

Winners Dog and Reserve Winners Bitch, which could be awarded the points in the case of a disqualification. The Winners Dog and Winners Bitch, the two that are awarded the points for the breed, then compete with any champions of record (often called "specials") entered in the show. The judge reviews the Winners Dog, Winners Bitch and all of the champions to select his Best of Breed. The Best of Winners is selected between the Winners Dog and Winners Bitch. Were one of these two to be selected Best of Breed, he or she would automatically be named Best of Winners as well. Finally, the judge selects his Best of Opposite Sex to the Best of Breed winner.

At a Group show or all-breed show, the Best of Breed winners from each breed then compete against one another for Group One through Group Four. The judge compares each Best of Breed to his breed standard, and the dog that most closely lives up to the ideal for his breed is selected as Group One. Finally, all seven group winners (from the Terrier Group, Toy Group, Hound Group, etc.) compete for Best in Show.

To find out about dog shows in your area, you can subscribe to the American Kennel Club's monthly magazine, the *American Kennel Gazette* and the accompanying *Events Calendar*. You can also look in your local newspaper for advertisements for dog shows in your area or go on the Internet to the AKC's website, www.akc.org.

If your Stafford is six months of age or older and registered with the AKC, you can enter him in a dog show where the breed is offered classes. Provided that your Stafford does not have a disqualifying fault, he can compete. Only unaltered dogs can be entered in a dog show, so if you have spayed or neutered your Stafford, your dog cannot compete in conformation shows. The reason for this is simple. Dog shows are the main forum to prove which representatives in a breed are worthy of being bred. Only dogs that have achieved championships—the AKC "seal of approval" for quality in pure-bred dogs—should be bred. Altered dogs, however, can participate in other AKC events such as obedience trials and the Canine Good Citizen® program.

Before you actually step into the ring, you would be well advised to sit back and observe the judge's ring procedure. If it is your first time in the ring, do not be over-anxious and run to the front of the line. It is much better to stand back and study how the exhibitor in front of you is performing. The judge asks each handler to "stack" the dog, hopefully showing the dog off to his best advantage. The judge will observe the dog from a distance and from different angles, and approach the dog to check his teeth, overall structure, alertness and muscle tone, as well as consider how well the dog "conforms" to the standard. Most importantly, the judge will have the exhibitor move the dog around the ring in some pattern that he should specify (another advantage to not going first, but always listen since some judges change their directions—and the judge is always right!). Finally, the judge will give the dog one last look before moving on to the next exhibitor.

If you are not in the top four in your class at your first show, do not be discouraged. Be patient and consistent, and you may eventually find yourself in a winning line-up. Remember that the winners were once in your shoes and have devoted many hours and much money to earn the placement. If you find that your dog is losing every time and never getting a nod, it may be time to consider a different dog sport or to just enjoy your Staffordshire Bull Terrier as a pet.

Parent clubs offer other events, such as agility, obedience, fun events and more, which may be of interest to the owner of a well-trained Stafford.

OBEDIENCE TRIALS

Obedience trials in the US trace back to the early 1930s when organized obedience training was developed to demonstrate how well dog and owner could work together. The pioneer of obedience trials is Mrs. Helen Whitehouse Walker, a Standard Poodle fancier, who designed a series of exercises after the Associated Sheep, Police, Army Dog Society of Great Britain. Since the days of Mrs. Walker, obedience trials have grown by leaps and bounds, and today there are over 2,000 trials held in the US every year, with more than 100,000 dogs competing. Any registered AKC dog can enter an obedience trial, regardless of conformational disqualifications or neutering.

Obedience trials are divided into three levels of progressive difficulty. At the first level, the Novice, dogs compete for the title Companion Dog (CD); at the intermediate level, the Open, dogs compete for the title Companion Dog Excellent (CDX); and at the advanced level, the Utility, dogs compete for the title Utility Dog (UD). Classes are sub-divided into "A" (for beginners) and "B" (for more experienced handlers). A perfect score at any level is 200, and a dog must score 170 or better to earn a "leg," of which three are needed to earn the title. To earn points, the dog must score more than 50% of the available points in each exercise; the possible points range from 20 to 40.

Each level consists of a different set of exercises. In the Novice level, the dog must heel on- and off-lead, come, long sit, long down and stand for examination. These skills are the basic ones required for a well-behaved "Companion Dog." The Open

---

SHOW-RING ETIQUETTE

Just as with anything else, there is a certain etiquette to the show ring that can only be learned through experience. Showing your dog can be quite intimidating to you as a novice when it seems as if everyone else knows what he is doing. You can familiarize yourself with ring procedure beforehand by taking showing classes to prepare you and your dog for conformation showing and by talking with experienced handlers. When you are in the ring, it is very important to pay attention and listen to the instructions you are given by the judge about where to move your dog. Remember, even the most skilled handlers had to start somewhere. Keep it up and you too will become a proficient handler as you gain practice and experience.

level requires that the dog perform the same exercises as in the Novice, but without a leash for extended lengths of time, as well as retrieve a dumbbell, broad jump and drop on recall. In the Utility level, dogs must perform ten difficult exercises, including scent discrimination, hand signals for basic commands, directed jump and directed retrieve.

Once a dog has earned the UD title, he can compete with other proven obedience dogs for the coveted title of Utility Dog Excellent (UDX), which requires that the dog win "legs" in ten shows. Utility Dogs who earn "legs" in Open B and Utility B earn points toward their Obedience Trial Champion title. In 1977, the title Obedience Trial Champion (OTCh.) was established by the AKC. To become an OTCh., a dog needs to earn 100 points, which requires three first places in Open B and Utility under three different judges.

The Grand Prix of obedience trials, the AKC National Obedience Invitational gives qualifying Utility Dogs the chance to win the newest and highest title: National Obedience Champion (NOC). Only the top 25 ranked obedience dogs, plus any dog ranked in the top 3 in his breed, are allowed to compete.

AGILITY TRIALS

Having had its origins in the UK back in 1977, AKC agility had its official beginning in the US in August 1994, when the first licensed agility trials were held. The AKC allows all registered breeds (including Miscellaneous Class breeds) to participate, providing the dog is 12 months of age or older. Agility is designed so that the handler demonstrates how well the dog can work at his side. The handler directs his dog over an obstacle course that includes jumps as well as tires, the dog walk, weave poles, pipe tunnels, collapsed tunnels, etc. While working his way through the course, the dog must keep one eye and ear on the handler and the rest of his body on the course. The handler gives verbal and hand signals to guide the dog through the course.

The first organization to

Staffordshire Bull Terriers usually do well in agility trials because they are exceptionally athletic and attentive to their handlers, and they surely love the exercise.

promote agility trials in the US was the United States Dog Agility Association, Inc. (USDAA), which was established in 1986 and spawned numerous member clubs around the country. Both the USDAA and the AKC offer titles to winning dogs. Three

NO SHOW

Never show a dog that is sick or recovering from surgery or infection. Not only will this put your own dog under a tremendous amount of stress, but you will also put other dogs at risk of contracting any illness your dog has. Likewise, bitches who are in heat will distract and disrupt the performances of males who are competing, and bitches that are pregnant will likely be stressed and exhausted by a long day of showing.

titles are available through the USDAA: Agility Dog (AD), Advanced Agility Dog (AAD) and Master Agility Dog (MAD). The AKC offers Novice Agility (NA), Open Agility (OA), Agility Excellent (AX) and Master Agility Excellent (MX). Beyond these four AKC titles, dogs can win additional ones in "jumper" classes, Jumpers with Weave Novice (NAJ), Open (OAJ) and Excellent (MXJ), which lead to the ultimate title(s): MACH, Master Agility Champion. Dogs can continue to add number designations to the MACH titles, indicating how many times the dog has met the MACH requirements, such as MACH1, MACH2 and so on.

Agility is great fun for dog and owner with many rewards for everyone involved. If you are interested in giving it a try, you should join a training club that has obstacles and experienced agility handlers who can introduce you and your dog to the "ropes" (and tires, tunnels, etc.).

TRACKING

Any dog is capable of tracking, using his nose to follow a trail. Tracking tests are exciting and competitive ways to test your Stafford's instinctive scenting ability and his ability to search and rescue. The AKC started tracking tests in 1937, when the first AKC-licensed test took place

as part of the Utility level at an obedience trial. Ten years later in 1947, the AKC offered the first title, Tracking Dog (TD). It was not until 1980 that the AKC added the title Tracking Dog Excellent (TDX), which was followed by the title Versatile Surface Tracking (VST) in 1995. The title Champion Tracker (CT) is awarded to a dog who has earned all three titles.

In the beginning level of tracking, the owner follows the dog through a field on a long lead. To earn the TD title, the dog must follow a track laid by a human 30 to 120 minutes prior. The track is about 500 yards with up to 5 directional changes. The TDX requires that the dog follow a track that is 3 to 5 hours old over a course up to 1,000 yards with up to 7 directional changes. The VST requires that the dog follow a track up to 5 hours old through an urban setting.

TEMPERAMENT PLUS
Although it seems that physical conformation is the only factor considered in the show ring, temperament is also of utmost importance. An aggressive or fearful dog should not be shown, as bad behavior will not be tolerated and may pose a threat to the judge, other exhibitors, you and your dog.

BEHAVIOR OF THE
STAFFORDSHIRE BULL TERRIER

As a Staffordshire Bull Terrier owner, you have selected your dog so that you and your loved ones can have a companion, a protector, a friend and a four-legged family member. You invest time, money and effort to care for and train the family's new charge. Of course, this chosen canine behaves perfectly! Well, perfectly like a *dog*.

THINK LIKE A DOG

Dogs do not think like humans, nor do humans think like dogs, though we try. Unfortunately, a dog is incapable of figuring out how humans think, so the responsibility falls on the owner to adopt a viable canine mindset. Dogs cannot rationalize, and they exist in the present moment. Many a dog owner makes the mistake in training of thinking that he can reprimand his dog for something the dog did a while ago. Basically, you cannot even reprimand a dog for something he did 20 seconds ago! Either catch him in the act or forget it! It is a waste of your and your dog's time—in his mind, you are reprimanding him for whatever he is doing at that moment.

The following behavioral problems represent some that owners most commonly encounter. Every dog is unique and every situation is unique. No author could purport for you to solve your Stafford's problem simply by reading a chapter. Here we outline some basic "dogspeak" so that owners' chances of solving behavioral problems are increased. Discuss bad habits with your veterinarian and he can recommend a behavioral specialist to consult in appropriate cases. Since behavioral abnormalities are the leading reason for owners' abandoning their pets, we hope that you will make a valiant effort to solve your Stafford's problem. Patience and

POLITE PLAY

Physical games like pulling contests, wrestling, jumping and teasing should not be encouraged. Inciting a dog's crazy behavior tends to confuse him. The owner has to be able to control his dog at all times. Even in play, your dog has to know that you are the leader and that you decide when to play and when to settle down.

understanding are virtues that must dwell in every pet-loving household.

AGGRESSION

This is the most obvious problem that concerns owners of Staffordshire Bull Terriers. Aggression can be a very big problem in dogs, but more so in a breed with a fighting background. Aggression, when not controlled, always becomes dangerous. An aggressive dog, no matter the size, may lunge at, bite or even attack a person or another dog, although the Stafford is unlikely to attack a human unless irresponsibly trained.

Aggressive behavior is not to be tolerated. It is more than just inappropriate behavior; it is not safe, especially with a tenacious, powerful breed such as the Stafford. It is painful for a family to watch their dog become unpredictable in his behavior to the point where they are afraid of him. While not all aggressive behavior is dangerous, things like growling, baring teeth, etc., can be frightening. It is important to ascertain why the dog is acting in this manner. Aggression is a display of dominance, and the dog should not have the dominant role in his pack, which is, in this case, your family.

It is important not to challenge an aggressive dog, as this could provoke an attack. Observe your

Stafford's body language. Does he make direct eye contact and stare? Does he try to make himself as large as possible: ears pricked, chest out, tail erect? Height and size signify authority in a dog pack—being taller or "above" another dog literally means that he is "above" in the social status. These body signals tell you that your Stafford thinks he is in charge, a problem that needs to be addressed. An aggressive dog is unpredictable. You never know when he is going to strike and what he is going to do. You cannot understand why a dog that is playful and loving one minute is growling and snapping the next.

Fear is a common cause of

Some Staffords become aggressive when meeting other dogs if they feel that their leadership is being challenged.

AIN'T MISBEHAVIN'

Punishment is rarely necessary for a misbehaving dog. Dogs that habitually behave badly probably had a poor education and do not know what is expected of them. They need training. Negative reinforcement on your part usually does more harm than good.

being gentle and by supervising his interactions, you are showing him that there is no need to be afraid or defensive.

The best solution is to consult a behavioral specialist, one who has experience with the Staffordshire Bull Terrier if possible. Together, perhaps you can pinpoint the cause of your dog's aggression and do something about it. An aggressive dog cannot be trusted, and a dog that cannot be trusted is not safe to have as a family pet. If the pet Stafford becomes untrustworthy, he cannot be kept in the home with the family, so the family must get rid of the dog. In the *very* worst case, euthanasia might be considered.

aggression in dogs. If you can isolate what brings out the fear reaction, you can help the dog get over it. Supervise your Stafford's interactions with people and other dogs, and praise the dog when it goes well. If he starts to act aggressively in a situation, correct him and remove him from the situation. Do not let people approach the dog and start petting him without your express permission. That way, you can have the dog sit to accept petting, and praise him when he behaves properly. You are focusing on praise and on modifying his behavior by rewarding him when he acts appropriately. By

AGGRESSION TOWARD OTHER DOGS
In general, a dog's aggressive behavior toward another dog stems from not enough exposure to other dogs at an early age. In Staffords, early socialization with other dogs is absolutely essential. Staffords are naturally aggressive toward other dogs: they were bred to be "anti-dog." It's the breeder's and owner's responsibility to curb and redirect this aggression so that the Stafford can become an upright member of canine society.

If other dogs make your Stafford nervous and agitated, he will lash out as a defensive mechanism. A dog who has not received sufficient exposure to other canines tends to believe that he is

Play between dogs rarely turns into aggression. This dam is playing with her pup and teaching the youngster a lesson in pack order at the same time.

the only dog on the planet. The animal becomes so dominant that he does not even show signs that he is fearful or threatened. Without growling or any other physical signal as a warning, he will lunge at and bite the other dog.

A way to correct this is to let your Stafford approach another dog when walking on leash. Watch very closely and, at the very first sign of aggression, correct your Stafford and pull him away. Scold him for any sign of discomfort, and then praise him when he ignores or tolerates the other dog. Keep this up until he stops the aggressive behavior, learns to ignore the other dog or even accepts other dogs. Praise him lavishly for this correct behavior.

DOMINANT AGGRESSION

A social hierarchy is firmly established in a wild dog pack. The dog wants to dominate those under him and please those above him. Dogs know that there must be a leader. If you are not the obvious choice for emperor, the dog will

---

DOGGIE DEMOCRACY

Your dog inherited the pack-leader mentality. He only knows about pecking order. He instinctively wants to be "top dog," but you have to convince him that you are boss. There is no such thing as living in a democracy with your dog. You are the one who makes the rules.

---

assume the throne! These conflicting innate desires are what a dog owner is up against when he sets about training a dog. In training a dog to obey commands, the owner is reinforcing that he is the top dog in the "pack" and that the dog should, and should want to, serve his superior. Thus, the owner is suppressing the dog's urge to dominate by modifying his behavior and making him obedient.

An important part of training is taking every opportunity to reinforce that you are the leader. The simple action of making your Stafford sit to wait for his food instead of allowing him to run up to get it when he wants it says that you control when he eats and that he is dependent on you for food. Although it may be difficult, do not give in to your dog's wishes every time he whines at you or looks at you with pleading eyes. It is a constant effort to show the dog that his place in the pack is at the bottom.

This is not meant to sound cruel or inhumane. You love your Stafford and you should treat him with care and affection. Dog training is not about being cruel, it is about molding the dog's behavior into what is acceptable and teaching your dog to live by your rules. In theory, it is quite simple: catch him in appropriate behavior and reward him for it. Add a dog into the equation and it becomes a bit more trying, but, as a rule of

> ### FEAR IN A GROWN DOG
> Fear in a grown dog is often the result of improper or incomplete socialization as a pup, or it can be the result of a traumatic experience he suffered when young. Keep in mind that the term "traumatic" is relative—something that you would not think twice about can leave a lasting negative impression on a puppy. If the dog experiences a similar experience later in life, he may try to fight back to protect himself. Again, this behavior is very unpredictable, especially if you do not know what is triggering his fear.

thumb, positive reinforcement is what works best.

With a dominant dog, punishment and negative reinforcement can have the opposite effect of what you are after. It can make a dog fearful and/or act out aggressively if he feels he is being challenged. Remember, a dominant dog perceives himself at the top of the social heap and will fight to defend his perceived status. The best way to prevent that is never to give him reason to think that he is in control in the first place.

If you are having trouble training your Stafford and it seems as if he is constantly challenging your authority, seek the help of an obedience trainer or behavioral specialist. A professional will work with both you and your dog to teach you effective techniques to use at home. Beware of trainers who rely on excessively harsh methods; scolding is necessary now and then, but the focus in your training should *always* be on positive reinforcement.

SEXUAL BEHAVIOR
Dogs exhibit certain sexual behaviors that may have influenced your choice of male or female when you first purchased your Staffordshire Bull Terrier. Spaying/neutering will eliminate these behaviors, but if you are purchasing a dog that you wish to breed, you should be aware of what you will have to deal with throughout the dog's life.

Female dogs usually have two estruses per year, with each season lasting about three weeks. These are the only times in which a female dog will mate, and she usually will not allow this until the second week of the cycle. If a bitch is not bred during the heat cycle, it is not uncommon for her to experience a false pregnancy, in which her mammary glands swell and she exhibits maternal tendencies toward toys or other objects.

With male dogs, owners must be aware that whole dogs (dogs who are not neutered) have the natural inclination to mark their territory. Males mark their territory by spraying small amounts of urine as they lift their legs in a macho ritual. Marking can occur both outdoors in the yard and around the neighborhood as well as indoors on furniture legs, curtains and the sofa. Such behavior can be very frustrating for the owner; early training is strongly urged before the "urge" strikes your dog. Neutering the male at an appropriate early age can solve this problem before it becomes a habit.

Other problems associated with males are wandering and mounting. Both of these habits, of course, belong to the unneutered dog, whose sexual drive leads him away from home in search of the bitch in heat. Males will mount females in heat, as well as any other dog, male or female, that happens to catch their fancy. Other possible mounting partners include his owner, the furniture, guests to the home and strangers on the street. Discourage such behavior early on.

Owners must further recognize that mounting is not merely a sexual expression but also one of dominance, seen in males and females alike. Be consistent and persistent and you will find that you can "move mounters."

CHEWING

The national canine pastime is chewing! Every dog loves to sink his "canines" into a tasty bone, but if a bone is not available, almost anything will do! Dogs need to chew, to massage their gums, to make their new teeth feel better and to exercise their jaws. This is a natural behavior deeply imbedded in all things canine. Our role as owners is not to stop chewing, but to redirect it to positive, chew-worthy objects. Be an informed owner and purchase proper chew toys like strong nylon bones made for large dogs for your Stafford. Be sure that the devices are safe and durable, since your dog's safety is at risk. Again, the owner is responsible for ensuring a dog-proof environment.

The best answer is prevention: that is, put your shoes, handbags and other tasty objects in their proper places (out of the reach of the growing canine mouth). Direct your puppy to his toys whenever you see him tasting the furniture legs or your pant leg. Make a loud noise to attract the pup's attention

Staffordshire Bull Terriers have strong jaws and teeth. They can destroy many types of dog toys in short order. Use only toys made specifically to be indestructible.

and immediately escort him to his chew toy and engage him with the toy for at least four minutes, praising and encouraging him all the while.

Some trainers recommend deterrents, such as hot pepper or another bitter spice or a product designed for this purpose, to discourage the dog from chewing on unwanted objects. This is sometimes reliable, but you should test out a small amount of the product with your own dog before investing in a case of it.

JUMPING UP

Jumping up is a dog's friendly way of saying hello! Some dog owners do not mind when their dog jumps up, which is fine for them. The problem arises when guests come to the house and the dog greets them in the same manner—whether they like it or not! However friendly the greeting may be, chances are your visitors will

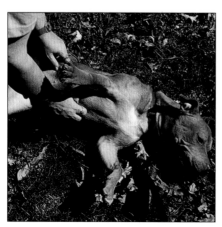

Scratch his belly and watch him smile! Staffords have a real sense of humor and a real love of their owners.

not appreciate being knocked over by your boisterous Stafford. The dog will not be able to distinguish upon whom he can jump and whom he cannot. Therefore, it is probably best to discourage this behavior entirely.

Pick a command such as "Off" (avoid using "Down" since you will use that for the dog to lie down) and tell him "Off" when he jumps up. Place him on the ground on all fours and have him sit, praising him the whole time. Always lavish him with praise and petting when he is in the sit position. This way, you are instilling polite behavior while still giving him a warm affectionate greeting, because you are as excited to see him as he is to see you!

DIGGING

Digging, which is seen as a destructive behavior to humans, is actually quite a natural behavior in dogs. Since your Stafford is part "earth dog" (also known as terrier), his desire to dig can be irrepressible and most frustrating to his owners. When digging occurs in your yard, it is actually a normal behavior redirected into something the dog can do in his everyday life. In the wild, a dog would be actively seeking food, making his own shelter, etc. He would be using his paws in a purposeful manner for his survival. Since you provide him with food and shelter, he has no need to use his paws for these purposes, and so the energy that he would be using manifests itself in the form of holes all over your yard and flower beds.

Perhaps your dog is digging as a reaction to boredom—it is somewhat similar to someone eating a whole bag of chips in front of the television—because they are there and there is not anything better to do! Basically, the answer is to provide the dog with adequate play and exercise so that his mind and paws are occupied, and so that he feels as if he is doing something useful.

Of course, digging is easiest to control if it is stopped as soon as possible, but it is often hard to catch a dog in the act, especially if he is alone in the yard during the day. If your dog is a compulsive digger and is not easily distracted by other activities, you can designate an area on your property where it is okay for him to dig. If you catch him digging in an off-limits area of the yard, immediately bring him to the approved area and praise him for digging there. Keep a close eye on him so that you can catch him as that is the only way he is going to understand what is permitted and what is not. If you bring him to a hole he dug an hour ago and tell him "No," he will understand that you are not fond of holes, dirt or flowers. If you catch him while he is stifle-deep in your tulips, that is when he will get your message.

SMILE!
Dogs and humans may be the only animals that smile. A dog will imitate the smile on his owner's face when he greets a friend. The dog only smiles at his human friends; he never smiles at another dog or cat. Usually, a dog rolls up his lips and shows his teeth in a clenched mouth while rolling over onto his back, begging for a soft scratch.

BARKING

Dogs cannot talk—oh, what they would say if they could! Instead, barking is a dog's way of "talking." It can be somewhat frustrating because it is not always easy to tell what a dog means by his bark—is he excited, happy, frightened or angry? Whatever it is that the dog is trying to say, he should not be punished for barking. Only when the barking becomes excessive, and when the excessive barking becomes a bad habit, does the behavior need to be modified. Fortunately, Staffords are not as vocal as most other terriers, and they tend to use their barks more purposefully than most dogs. If an intruder came into your home in the middle of the night and your Stafford barked a warning, wouldn't you be pleased? You would probably deem your dog a hero, a wonderful guardian and protector of the home.

Most dogs, however, are not as discriminate as the Stafford. For instance, if a friend drops by unexpectedly and rings the doorbell and is greeted with a sudden sharp bark, you would probably be annoyed at the dog. But in reality, isn't this just the same behavior? The dog does not know any better...unless he sees who is at the door and it is someone he knows, he will bark as a means of vocalizing that his (and your)

This Stafford jumped up and stole the child's biscuit. Children should always be supervised when in the company of dogs, especially when the child has a tasty tidbit!

territory is being threatened. While your friend is not posing a threat, it is all the same to the dog. Barking is his means of letting you know that there is an intrusion, whether friend or foe, on your property. This type of barking is instinctive and should not be discouraged.

Excessive habitual barking, however, is a problem that should be corrected early on. As your Stafford grows up, you will be able to tell when his barking is purposeful and when it is for no reason. You will become able to distinguish your dog's different barks and their meanings. For example, the bark when someone comes to the door will be different from the bark when he is excited to see you. It is similar to a person's tone of voice, except that the dog has to rely totally on tone of voice because he does not have the benefit of using words. An incessant barker will be evident at an early age.

There are some things that encourage a dog to bark. For example, if your dog barks non-stop for a few minutes and you give him a treat to quiet him, he believes that you are rewarding him for barking. He will associate barking with getting a treat, and will keep doing it until he is rewarded. If you give a "Quiet" command and reward him *after* he is quiet, he will begin to understand that silence is golden!

FOOD STEALING

Is your dog devising ways of stealing food from your countertop or coffee table? If so, you must answer the following questions: Is your Stafford hungry, or is he "constantly famished" like every other chow hound? Why is there food out within the dogs reach in the first place? Face it, some dogs are more food-motivated than others; some dogs always seem hungry and can only think of their next meal. Food stealing is terrific fun and always yields a great reward—*food*, glorious food.

Begging and food stealing must never be tolerated from your dog. Your Stafford may be as clever and industrious as this fellow, who's learned to open the kitchen cabinets. This type of snooping could also lead to danger.

The owner's goal, therefore, is to make the "reward" less rewarding, even startling! Plant a shaker can (an empty soda can with coins inside) on the counter so that it catches your pooch off-guard. There are other devices available that will surprise the dog when he is looking for a mid-afternoon snack. Such remote-control devices, though not the first choice of some trainers, allow the correction to come from the object instead of the owner. These devices are also useful to keep the snacking hound from napping on furniture that is forbidden. Of course, not putting food where the dog can steal it will prevent the problem altogether.

BEGGING

Just like food stealing, begging is a favorite pastime of hungry puppies! It yields that same reward—*food!* Dogs quickly learn that their owners keep the "good food" for themselves, and that we humans do not dine on kibble alone. Begging is a conditioned response related to a specific stimulus, time and place. The sounds of the kitchen, cans and bottles opening, crinkling bags, the smell of food in preparation, etc., will excite the chow hound and soon the paws are in the air!

Here is the solution to stopping this behavior: Never give into a beggar! You are rewarding the dog for sitting pretty, jumping up, whining and rubbing his nose into you by giving him that glorious reward—*food*. By ignoring the dog, you will (eventually) force the behavior into extinction. Note that the behavior likely gets worse before it disappears, so be sure there are not any "softies" in the family who will give in to little

"Oliver" every time he whimpers, "More, please."

SEPARATION ANXIETY

Your Stafford may howl, whine or otherwise vocalize his displeasure at your leaving the house and his being left alone. This is a case of separation anxiety, and there are things that can be done to eliminate this problem. Your dog needs to learn that he will be fine on his own for a while and that he will not wither away if you are not by his side. In fact, constant attention can lead to separation anxiety in the first place. If you are endlessly coddling and cooing over your dog, he will come to expect this from you all of the time and it will be more traumatic for him when you are not there. Obviously, you enjoy spending time with your dog, and he thrives on your love and attention. However, it should not become a dependent relationship in which he is heartbroken without you.

One thing you can do to minimize separation anxiety is to make your entrances and exits as low-key as possible. Do not give your dog a long drawn-out goodbye, and do not lavish him with hugs and kisses when you return. This is giving in to the attention that he craves, and it will only make him miss it more when you are away. Another thing you can try is to give your dog a treat when you leave; this will not only keep him occupied and keep his mind off the fact that you just left, but it will also help him associate your leaving with a pleasant experience.

You may have to accustom your dog to being left alone in intervals, much like when you introduced your pup to his crate. Of course, when your dog starts whimpering as you approach the door, your first instinct will be to run to him and comfort him, but do not do it! Eventually he will adjust and be just fine if you take it in small steps. His anxiety stems from being placed in an unfamiliar situation; by familiarizing him with being alone, he will learn that he is okay. That is not to say you should purposely leave your dog home alone, but the dog needs to know that, while he can depend on you for his care, you do not have to be by his side 24 hours a day.

When the dog is alone in the house, he should be confined to

I'M HOME!
Dogs left alone for varying lengths of time may often react wildly when their owners return. Sometimes they run, jump, bite, chew, tear things apart, wet themselves, gobble their food or behave in very undisciplined ways. If your dog behaves in this manner upon your return home, allow him to calm down before greeting him or he will consider your attention as a reward for his antics.

his crate or a designated dog-proof area of the house. This should be the area in which he sleeps and already feels comfortable so he will feel more at ease when he is alone. This is just one of the many examples in which a crate is an invaluable tool for you and your dog, and another reinforcement of why your dog should view his crate as a "happy" place, a place of his own.

COPROPHAGIA

Feces eating is, to most humans, one of the most disgusting behaviors that their dog could engage in, yet to the dog it is perfectly normal. It is hard for us to understand why a dog would want to eat his own feces. He could be seeking certain nutrients that are missing from his diet, he could be just plain hungry or he could be attracted by the pleasing (to a dog) scent. While coprophagia most often refers to the dog eating his own feces, a dog may eat that of another animal as well if he comes across it. For example, dogs often find the stool of cats and horses more palatable than that of other dogs.

Veterinarians have found that diets with a low digestibility, containing relatively low levels of fiber and high levels of starch, increase coprophagia. Therefore, high-fiber diets may decrease the likelihood of dogs' eating feces. Both the consistency of the stool (how firm it feels in the dog's

mouth) and the presence of undigested nutrients increase the likelihood. Once the dog develops diarrhea from feces eating, it will likely quit this distasteful habit, since dogs tend to prefer eating harder feces.

To discourage this behavior, first make sure that the food you are feeding your dog is nutritionally complete and that he is getting enough food. If changes in his diet do not seem to work, and no medical cause can be found, you will have to modify the behavior before it becomes a habit through environmental control. There are some tricks you can try, such as adding something to the dog's food that will make his feces unpleasant-tasting after passing through the dog. Of course, the best way to prevent your dog from eating his stool is to make it unavailable— clean up after he eliminates and remove any stool from the yard. If it is not there, he cannot eat it, so you will not have a problem.

Never reprimand the dog for stool eating, as this rarely impresses the dog. Veterinarians recommend distracting the dog while he is in the act of stool eating. Another option is to muzzle the dog when he is in the yard to relieve himself; this usually is effective within 30 to 60 days. Coprophagia is seen most frequently in pups 6 to 12 months of age and usually disappears around the dog's first birthday.

INDEX

Page numbers in **boldface** indicate illustrations.

My Staffordshire Bull Terrier

PUT YOUR PUPPY'S FIRST PICTURE HERE

Dog's Name _____

Date _____ Photographer _____